Formative Assessment & Standards-Based Grading

Robert J. Marzano

Marzano Research Laboratory
Powered by Solution Tree

CLASSROOM STRATEGIES **THAT** WORK

555 North Morton Street
Bloomington, IN 47404

888.849.0851
FAX: 866.801.1447

email: info@marzanoresearch.com
marzanoresearch.com

Visit **marzanoresearch.com/classroomstrategiesthatwork** to download reproducibles in this book.

Printed in the United States of America

Library of Congress Control Number: 2009908602

ISBN: 978-0-9822592-2-1 (paperback)
       978-0-9822592-3-8 (library binding)

13 12 11 10 09   1 2 3 4 5

FSC
Mixed Sources
Product group from well-managed
forests and other controlled sources
Cert no. SW-COC-002283
www.fsc.org
© 1996 Forest Stewardship Council

Director of Production: Gretchen Knapp

Managing Production Editor: Caroline Wise

Senior Production Editor: Risë Koben

Copy Editor: R. C. Gokulakrishnan

Proofreader: Sarah Payne-Mills

Indexer: Abella

Text Designer: Amy Shock

Compositor: Quick Sort India Private Ltd.

Cover Designer: Pamela Rude

MARZANO RESEARCH LABORATORY DEVELOPMENT TEAM

Staff Writer

Lindsay A. Carleton

Marzano Research Laboratory Associates

Chris Briggs-Hale

Jane K. Doty Fischer

Maria C. Foseid

Mark P. Foseid

Tammy Heflebower

Edie Holcomb

Sharon Kramer

David Livingston

Beatrice McGarvey

Diane E. Paynter

Debra Pickering

Salle Quackenboss

Tom Roy

ACKNOWLEDGMENTS

Marzano Research Laboratory would like to thank the following reviewers:

Larry Ainsworth
Executive Director, Professional Development
The Leadership and Learning Center
Englewood, Colorado

Susan M. Brookhart
Consultant
Brookhart Enterprises
Helena, Montana

Kay Burke
President
Kay Burke and Associates
Greensboro, Georgia

Tony Frontier
Associate Professor
Cardinal Stritch University
Milwaukee, Wisconsin

Douglas B. Reeves
Chairman
The Leadership and Learning Center
Salem, Massachusetts

Mike Schmoker
Author and Consultant
Flagstaff, Arizona

Visit **marzanoresearch.com/classroomstrategiesthatwork**
to download reproducibles from this book.

CONTENTS

Italicized entries indicate reproducible pages.

CHAPTER 3

THE NEED FOR A NEW SCALE 39

CHAPTER 4

DESIGNING ASSESSMENTS 59

CHAPTER **5**

TRACKING STUDENT PROGRESS 81

CHAPTER **6**

GRADING AND REPORTING 105

EPILOGUE 129

ABOUT THE AUTHOR

 Dr. Robert J. Marzano is the cofounder and CEO of Marzano Research Laboratory in Denver, Colorado. Throughout his forty years in the field of education, he has become a speaker, trainer, and author of more than thirty books and 150 articles on topics such as instruction, assessment, writing and implementing standards, cognition, effective leadership, and school intervention. His books include: *The Art and Science of Teaching: A Comprehensive Framework for Effective Instruction, Making Standards Useful in the Classroom, District Leadership That Works: Striking the Right Balance, Designing and Teaching Learning Goals and Objectives,* and *On Excellence in Teaching.* His practical translations of the most current research and theory into classroom strategies are internationally known and widely practiced by both teachers and administrators. He received a bachelor's degree from Iona College in New York, a master's degree from Seattle University, and a doctorate from the University of Washington.

ABOUT MARZANO RESEARCH LABORATORY

Marzano Research Laboratory (MRL) is a joint venture between Solution Tree and Dr. Robert J. Marzano. MRL combines Dr. Marzano's forty years of educational research with continuous action research in all major areas of schooling in order to provide effective and accessible instructional strategies, leadership strategies, and classroom assessment strategies that are always at the forefront of best practice. By providing such an all-inclusive research-into-practice resource center, MRL provides teachers and principals the tools they need to effect profound and immediate improvement in student achievement.

INTRODUCTION

Formative Assessment and Standards-Based Grading is the second in a series of books collectively referred to as the *Classroom Strategies That Work* library. The purpose of this series is to provide teachers as well as building and district administrators with an in-depth treatment of research-based instructional strategies that can be used in the classroom to enhance student achievement. Many of the strategies addressed in this series have been covered in other works such as *The Art and Science of Teaching: A Comprehensive Framework for Effective Instruction* (Marzano, 2007), *Classroom Assessment and Grading That Work* (Marzano, 2006), and *Classroom Instruction That Works* (Marzano, Pickering, & Pollock, 2001). Although those works devoted a chapter or a part of a chapter to particular strategies, the *Classroom Strategies That Work* library devotes an entire book to an instructional strategy or set of related strategies.

Designing effective assessments is critical for any teacher. In order to make judgments about the status of a student or an entire class at any given point in time, teachers need as much accurate data as possible about an individual student's progress, or the progress of the class as a whole, to determine their next instructional steps. As straightforward as this might sound, designing assessments, using them purposefully, and incorporating them into a system of overall grading take insight and practice. *Formative Assessment and Standards-Based Grading* addresses the misconceptions about formative assessment and how it can be used in an overall grading scheme.

We begin with a brief but inclusive chapter that reviews the research and theory on formative assessment, instructional feedback, and grading. Although you might skip this chapter and move right into those that provide recommendations for classroom practice, you are strongly encouraged to examine the research and theory, as it is the foundation for the entire book. Indeed, a basic purpose of *Formative Assessment and Standards-Based Grading* and other books in the *Classroom Strategies That Work* library is to present the most useful instructional strategies that are based on the strongest research and theory available.

Because research and theory can provide only a general direction for classroom practice, *Formative Assessment and Standards-Based Grading* (and each book in the series) goes one step further to translate that research into applications for the classroom. Specifically, it addresses misconceptions about formative assessment, provides formatively based classroom assessment strategies, and discusses in depth how those strategies can effect change in overall grading systems on both small and large scales. It is important to note, however, that individual teachers, schools, and districts must make necessary adaptations to meet the unique needs of their students.

How to Use This Book

Formative Assessment and Standards-Based Grading can be used as a self-study text that provides an in-depth understanding of how to design and interpret assessments and use those assessments to develop meaningful grades. As you progress through the chapters, you will encounter exercises. It is important to complete these exercises and then compare your answers with those in the back of the text. Such interaction provides a review of the content and allows you to examine how clearly you understand it.

Teams of teachers or an entire faculty that wishes to examine the topics of assessment and grading in depth may also use *Formative Assessment and Standards-Based Grading*. When this is the case, teacher teams should do the exercises independently and then compare their answers in small-group and large-group settings.

Chapter 1

RESEARCH AND THEORY

Assessment and grading are two of the most talked about and sometimes misunderstood aspects of K–12 education. *Formative Assessment and Standards-Based Grading* seeks to bring some clarity to one particular type of assessment—formative—and explore through recommendations how it interacts with traditional and nontraditional grading practices. In this chapter, we review the research and theory that underpin these recommendations. We begin by discussing feedback, the practice in which both assessment and grading have their roots.

Feedback

The topic of feedback and its effect on student achievement is of great interest to researchers and practitioners. In fact, studies on the relationship between the two are plentiful and span about three decades. In an effort to operationally define feedback, researchers John Hattie and Helen Timperley (2007) explained that its purpose is "to reduce discrepancies between current understandings and performance and a goal" (p. 86). Researcher Valerie Shute (2008) said feedback is "information communicated to the learner that is intended to modify his or her thinking or behavior for the purpose of improving learning" (p. 154).

Feedback can be given formally or informally in group or one-on-one settings. It can take a variety of forms. As the preceding definitions illustrate, its most important and dominant characteristic is that it informs the student, the teacher, and all other interested parties about how to best enhance student learning.

Table 1.1 (page 4) presents the results from a variety of studies on feedback. The first column lists the major studies that have been conducted since 1976. The last three columns are related. Critical to understanding exactly how they are related are the concepts of meta-analysis and effect size (ES). Appendix B (page 153) explains the concepts of meta-analysis and effect size in some depth. Briefly though, *meta-analysis* is a research technique for quantitatively synthesizing a series of studies on the same topic. For example, as table 1.1 indicates, Kluger and DeNisi (1996) synthesized findings from 607 studies on the effects of feedback interventions. Typically, meta-analytic studies report their findings in terms of average ESs (see the ES column in table 1.1). In the Kluger and DeNisi meta-analysis, the average ES is 0.41. An *effect size* tells you how many standard deviations larger (or smaller) the average score for a group of students who were exposed to a given strategy (in this case, feedback) is than the average score for a group of students who were not exposed to a given strategy (in this case, no feedback). In short, an ES tells you how powerful a strategy is; the larger the ES, the more the strategy increases student learning.

Table 1.1 Research Results for Feedback

Synthesis Study	Focus	Number of Effect Sizes (ESs)	Average ES	Percentile Gain
Bloom, 1976	General effects of feedback	8	1.47	43
Lysakowski & Walberg, 1981[a]	General effects of feedback	39	1.15	37
Lysakowski & Walberg, 1982	General effects of feedback	94	0.97	33
Yeany & Miller, 1983	Diagnostic feedback in science	49	0.55	21
Moin, 1986[b]	General effects of feedback	Not reported	0.29	11
Haller, Child, & Walberg, 1988[c]	General effects of feedback	115	0.71	26
Tenenbaum & Goldring, 1989	General effects of feedback	16	0.66	25
Bangert-Drowns, Kulik, Kulik, & Morgan, 1991	General effects of feedback	58	0.26	10
Kumar, 1991[d]	General effects of feedback	5	1.35	41
Azevedo & Bernard, 1995[e]	Immediate feedback in computer-based instruction	22	0.80	29
Kluger & DeNisi, 1996	Effects of feedback interventions	607	0.41	16
Walberg, 1999	General effects of feedback	20	0.94	33
Hattie, 1999[b]	General effects of feedback	5,755	0.95	33
Haas, 2005	General effects of feedback	19	0.55	21

[a] Reported in Fraser, Walberg, Welch, & Hattie, 1987.
[b] Reported in Hattie & Timperley, 2007.
[c] Feedback was embedded in general metacognitive strategies.
[d] The dependent variable was engagement.
[e] Reported in Hattie, 2009.

ESs are typically small numbers. However, small ESs can translate into big percentile gains. For example, the average ES of 0.41 calculated by Kluger and DeNisi (1996) translates into a 16 percentile point gain (see appendix B, page 153, for a detailed description of ESs and a chart that translates ES numbers into percentile gains). Another way of saying this is that a student at the 50th percentile in a class where feedback was not provided (an average student in that class) would be predicted to rise to the 66th percentile if he or she were provided with feedback.

Hattie and Timperley (2007) synthesized the most current and comprehensive research in feedback and summarized findings from twelve previous meta-analyses, incorporating 196 studies and 6,972 ESs. They calculated an overall average ES of 0.79 for feedback (translating to a 29 percentile point gain). As shown by Hattie (2009), this is twice the average ES of typical educational innovations. One study by Stuart Yeh (2008) revealed that students who received feedback completed more work with greater accuracy than students who did not receive feedback. Furthermore, when feedback was withdrawn from students who were receiving it, rates of accuracy and completion dropped.

Interestingly, though the evidence for the effectiveness of feedback has been quite strong, it has also been highly variable. For example, in their analyzing of more than six hundred experimental/control studies, Kluger and DeNisi (1996) found that in 38 percent of the studies they examined, feedback had a negative effect on student achievement. This, of course, raises the critically important questions, What are the characteristics of feedback that produce positive effects on student achievement, and what are the characteristics of feedback that produce negative effects? In partial answer to this question, Kluger and DeNisi found that negative feedback has an ES of negative 0.14. This translates into a predicted decrease in student achievement of 6 percentile points. In general, negative feedback is that which does not let students know how they can get better.

Hattie and Timperley (2007) calculated small ESs for feedback containing little task-focused information (punishment = 0.20; praise = 0.14) but large ESs for feedback that focused on information (cues = 1.10, reinforcement = 0.94). They argued that feedback regarding the task, the process, and self-regulation is often effective, whereas feedback regarding the self (often delivered as praise) typically does not enhance learning and achievement. Operationally, this means that feedback to students regarding how well a task is going (task), the process they are using to complete the task (process), or how well they are managing their own behavior (self-regulation) is often effective, but feedback that simply involves statements like "You're doing a good job" has little influence on student achievement. Hattie and Timperley's ultimate conclusion was:

> Learning can be enhanced to the degree that students share the challenging goals of learning, adopt self-assessment and evaluation strategies, and develop error detection procedures and heightened self-efficacy to tackle more challenging tasks leading to mastery and understanding of lessons. (p. 103)

Assessment

In K–12 classrooms, the most common form of feedback is an assessment. While the research and theory on feedback and assessment overlap to a great extent, in this section we consider the research and theory that is specific to assessment.

Research on Assessment

The research on the effects of assessments on student learning paints a positive picture. To illustrate, table 1.2 (page 6) provides a synthesis of a number of meta-analytic studies on the effects of assessment as reported by Hattie (2009).

Table 1.2 Meta-Analytic Studies on Assessment as Reported by Hattie (2009)

Synthesis Study	Focus	Number of Effect Sizes (ESs)	Average ES	Percentile Gain
Kulik, Kulik, & Bangert-Drowns, 1984	Frequency of assessment	19	0.42	16
Fuchs & Fuchs, 1986		34	0.28	11
Bangert-Drowns, Kulik, & Kulik, 1991		35	0.23	9
Gocmen, 2003		233	0.40	16
Kim, 2005[a]		644	0.39	15
		622	0.39	15
Lee, 2006		55	0.36	14
Hausknecht, Halpert, DiPaolo, & Gerrard, 2007		107	0.26	10
Menges & Brinko, 1986	General effects of assessment	31	0.44	17
Bangert-Drowns, Kulik, Kulik, & Morgan, 1991		58	0.26	10
Travlos & Pratt, 1995		17	0.71	26
Neubert, 1998		16	0.63	24
Swanson & Lussier, 2001		170	1.12	37
Witt, Wheeless, & Allen, 2006		81	1.15	37
Fuchs & Fuchs, 1986	Providing assessment feedback to teachers	21	0.70	26
Burns & Symington, 2002		57	1.10	36

[a] Two effect sizes are listed because of the differences in variables as reported by Hattie (2009). Readers should consult that study for more details.

Notice that table 1.2 is subdivided into three categories: frequency of assessment, general effects of assessment, and providing assessment feedback to teachers. The first category speaks to how frequently assessments are given. In general, student achievement benefits when assessments are given relatively frequently as opposed to infrequently. The study by Robert Bangert-Drowns, James Kulik, and Chen-Lin Kulik (1991) depicted in table 1.3 adds some interesting details to this generalization.

Note that in table 1.3, the effect of even one assessment in a fifteen-week period of time is substantial (0.34). Also note that there is a gradual increase in the size of the effect as the number of assessments increases. This trend should not be misconstrued as indicating that the more tests a teacher gives, the more students will achieve. As we shall see in subsequent chapters, a test is only one of many ways to obtain assessment data.

Table 1.3 Achievement Gain Associated With Number of Assessments Over Fifteen Weeks

Number of Assessments	Effect Size	Percentile Point Gain
0	0	0
1	0.34	13.5
5	0.53	20
10	0.60	22.5
15	0.66	24.5
20	0.71	26
25	0.78	28.5
30	0.82	29

Note: Effect sizes computed using data reported by Bangert-Drowns, Kulik, and Kulik (1991).

The second category in table 1.2, general effects of assessment, is the broadest and incorporates a variety of perspectives on assessment. Again, many of the specific findings in these studies manifest as the recommendations in subsequent chapters. Here it suffices to note that in the aggregate, these studies attest to the fact that properly executed assessments can be an effective tool for enhancing student learning.

The third category in table 1.2 deals with providing assessment feedback to teachers. Lynn Fuchs and Douglas Fuchs (1986) found that providing teachers with graphic representations of student progress was associated with an ES of 0.70, which translates into a 26 percentile point gain. This is quite consistent with a set of studies conducted at Marzano Research Laboratory in which teachers had students chart their progress on specific learning goals (Marzano Research Laboratory, 2009). The results are depicted in table 1.4.

Table 1.4 Studies on Students Tracking Their Progress

Study	Effect Size	Percentile Gain
1	2.44	49
2	3.66	49
3	1.50	43
4	-0.39	-15
5	0.75	27
6	1.00	34
7	0.07	3
8	1.68	45
9	0.07	3
10	1.20	38
11	-0.32	-13
12	0.43	17
13	0.84	30
14	0.63	24
Average	0.92	32

Table 1.4 reports the results of fourteen studies conducted by K–12 teachers on the effects of tracking student progress. The average ES of these fourteen studies was 0.92, which translates into a 32 percentile point gain. Taking these findings at face value, one would conclude that learning is enhanced when students track their own progress.

Note that in studies 4 and 11, tracking student progress had a negative effect on student achievement (indicated by the negative ES). As is the case with all assessment (and instructional) strategies, this strategy does not work equally well in all situations. Effective assessment requires ascertaining the correct way to use a strategy. In subsequent chapters, we make recommendations as to the correct way to track student progress.

Formative Assessments

Formative assessment has become very popular in the last decade. It is typically contrasted with summative assessment in that *summative assessments* are employed at the end of an instructional episode while *formative assessments* are used while instruction is occurring. As Susan Brookhart (2004, p. 45) explained, "Formative assessment means information gathered and reported for use in the development of knowledge and skills, and summative assessment means information gathered and reported for use in judging the outcome of that development."

Formative assessments became popular after Paul Black and Dylan Wiliam (1998a) summarized the findings from more than 250 studies on formative assessment. They saw ESs in those studies that ranged from 0.4 to 0.7 and drew the following conclusion:

> The research reported here shows conclusively that formative assessment does improve learning. The gains in achievement appear to be quite considerable, and as noted earlier, among the largest ever reported for educational interventions. As an illustration of just how big these gains are, an effect size of 0.7, if it could be achieved on a nationwide scale, would be equivalent to raising the mathematics attainment score of an "average" country like England, New Zealand, or the United States into the "top five" after the Pacific rim countries of Singapore, Korea, Japan, and Hong Kong. (p. 61)

In effect, Black and Wiliam were saying that an ES of 0.70 (the largest ES reported in the studies they summarized), when sustained for an entire nation, would dramatically enhance student achievement. Indeed, consulting the table in appendix B (page 155), we see that an ES of 0.70 is associated with a 26 percentile point gain in student achievement. The reporting of these findings captured the attention of U.S. educators.

The Black and Wiliam study is sometimes referenced as a meta-analysis of some 250 studies on formative assessment. As described in appendix B of this book, a meta-analysis is a quantitative synthesis of research in a specific area. When performing a meta-analysis, a researcher attempts to compute an average ES of a particular innovation (in this case, formative assessment) by examining all of the available studies. While Black and Wiliam certainly performed a rigorous analysis of the studies they examined, they did not conduct a traditional meta-analysis. In fact, in a section of their article titled "No Meta-Analysis," they explain, "It might seem desirable, and indeed might be anticipated as conventional, for a review of this type to attempt a meta-analysis of the quantitative studies that have been reported" (1998a, p. 52). They go on to note, however, that the 250 studies they examined were simply too different to compute an average ES.

It is important to keep two things in mind when considering the practice of formative assessment. The first is that, by definition, formative assessment is intimately tied to the formal and informal processes in classrooms. Stated differently, it would be a contradiction in terms to use "off the shelf" formative assessment designed by test makers. James Popham (2006) has harshly criticized the unquestioning use of commercially prepared formative assessments. He noted:

> As news of Black and Wiliam's conclusions gradually spread into faculty lounges, test publishers suddenly began to relabel many of their tests as "formative." This name-switching sales ploy was spurred on by the growing perception among educators that formative assessments could improve their students' test scores and help schools dodge the many accountability bullets being aimed their way. (p. 86)

To paraphrase Popham (2006), externally developed assessments simply do not meet the defining characteristics of formative assessment. Lorrie Shepard (2006) made the same point:

> The research-based concept of formative assessment, closely grounded in classroom instructional processes, has been taken over—hijacked—by commercial test publishers and is used instead to refer to formal testing systems called "benchmark" or "interim assessment systems." (as cited in Popham, 2006, p. 86)

A similar criticism might be leveled at many district-made "benchmark" assessments in that they frequently violate many of the basic assumptions underlying good formative assessment. As James McMillan (2007) explained:

> These tests, which are typically provided by the district or commercial test publishers, are administered on a regular basis to compare student achievement to "benchmarks" that indicate where student performance should be in relation to what is needed to do well on end-of-year high stakes tests. . . . Although the term *benchmark* is often used interchangeably with *formative* in the commercial testing market, there are important differences. Benchmark assessments are formal, structured tests that typically do not provide the level of detail needed for appropriate instructional correctives. (pp. 2–3)

The second thing to keep in mind is that while there is a good deal of agreement about its potential as a tool to enhance student achievement, the specifics of formative assessment are somewhat elusive. In fact, most descriptions of formative assessment are very general in nature. To illustrate, in their original study, Black and Wiliam (1998a) noted that "formative assessment does not have a tightly defined and widely accepted meaning" (p. 7). Dylan Wiliam and Siobhan Leahy (2007) described formative assessment as follows:

> The qualifier *formative* will refer not to an assessment or even to the purpose of an assessment, but rather to the function it actually serves. An assessment is formative to the extent that information from the assessment is fed back within the system and actually used to improve the performance of the system in some way (i.e., that the assessment *forms* the direction of improvement). (p. 31)

Rick Stiggins, Judith Arter, Jan Chappuis, and Stephen Chappuis (2006) described formative assessment as assessment *for* learning rather than assessment *of* learning:

> Assessments for learning happen while learning is still underway. These are the assessments that we conduct throughout teaching and learning to diagnose student needs, plan our next steps in instruction, provide students with feedback they can use to improve the quality of their work, and help students see and feel in control of their journey to success. . . . This is not about accountability—these are assessments *of* learning. This is about getting better. (p. 31)

Susan Brookhart and Anthony Nitko (2007) explained that "formative assessment is a loop: Students and teachers focus on a learning target, evaluate current student work against the target, act to move the work closer to the target, and repeat" (p. 116).

Along with these general descriptions, specifics regarding the practice of formative assessment have been offered. Unfortunately, there is no clear pattern of agreement regarding the specifics. For example, some advocates stress that formative assessments should not be recorded, whereas others believe they should. Some assert that formative assessments should not be considered when designing grades, where others see a place for them in determining a student's true final status (see O'Connor, 2002; Welsh & D'Agostino, 2009; Marzano, 2006). To a great extent, the purpose of this book is to articulate a well-crafted set of specifics regarding the practice of formative assessment.

Learning Progressions and Clear Goals

The development of learning progressions has become a prominent focus in the field of formative assessment. Margaret Heritage (2008) explained the link between learning progressions and formative assessment as follows:

> The purpose of formative assessment is to provide feedback to teachers and students during the course of learning about the gap between students' current and desired performance so that action can be taken to close the gap. To do this effectively, teachers need to have in mind a continuum of how learning develops in any particular knowledge domain so that they are able to locate students' current learning status and decide on pedagogical action to move students' learning forward. Learning progressions that clearly articulate a progression of learning in a domain can provide the big picture of what is to be learned, support instructional planning, and act as a touchstone for formative assessment. (p. 2)

One might think that learning progressions have already been articulated within the many state and national standards documents. This is not the case. Again, Heritage noted:

> Yet despite a plethora of standards and curricula, many teachers are unclear about how learning progresses in specific domains. This is an undesirable situation for teaching and learning, and one that particularly affects teachers' ability to engage in formative assessment. (p. 2)

The reason state and national standards are not good proxies for learning progressions is that they were not designed with learning progressions in mind. To illustrate, consider the following standard for grade 3 mathematics from the state of Washington (Washington Office of Superintendent of Public Instruction, 2008):

> Students will be able to round whole numbers through 10,000 to the nearest ten, hundred, and thousand. (p. 33)

This sample provides a fairly clear target of what students should know by grade 3, but it does not provide any guidance regarding the building blocks necessary to attain that goal. In contrast, Joan Herman and Kilchan Choi (2008, p. 7) provided a detailed picture of the nature of a learning progression relative to the concept of buoyancy. They identified the following levels (from highest to lowest) of understanding regarding the concept:

- Student knows that floating depends on having less density than the medium.

- Student knows that floating depends on having a small density.

- Student knows that floating depends on having a small mass and a large volume.

- Student knows that floating depends on having a small mass, or that floating depends on having a large volume.

- Student thinks that floating depends on having a small size, heft, or amount, or that it depends on being made out of a particular material.

- Student thinks that floating depends on being flat, hollow, filled with air, or having holes.

Obviously, with a well-articulated sequence of knowledge and skills like this, it is much easier to provide students with feedback as to their current status regarding a specific learning goal and what they must do to progress.

While one might characterize the work on learning progressions as relatively new and therefore relatively untested, it is related to a well-established and heavily researched area of curriculum design—learning goals. One might think of learning progressions as a series of related learning goals that culminate in the attainment of a more complex learning goal. Learning progressions can also be used to track student progress. The research on learning goals is quite extensive. Some of the more prominent studies are reported in table 1.5 (page 12).

Table 1.5 Research Results for Establishing Learning Goals

Synthesis Study	Focus	Number of Effect Sizes (ESs)	Average ES	Percentile Gain
Wise & Okey, 1983[a]	General effects of setting goals or objectives	3 25	1.37 0.48	41 18
Chidester & Grigsby, 1984[b]	Goal difficulty	21	0.44	17
Tubbs, 1986[c]	Goal difficulty	56	0.82	29
	Goal specificity	48	0.50	19
	Goal setting and feedback	3	0.56	21
	Participation in goal setting	17	0.002	0
Mento, Steel, & Karren, 1987[b]	Goal difficulty	118	0.58	22
Wood, Mento, & Locke, 1987[b]	Goal difficulty	72	0.58	22
	Goal specificity	53	0.43	17
Locke & Latham, 1990[c,d]	Goal difficulty	Not reported	0.52–0.82	20–29
	Goal specificity		0.42–0.80	16–29
Wright, 1990[b]	Goal difficulty	70	0.55	21
Lipsey & Wilson, 1993[e]	General effects of setting goals or objectives	204	0.55	21
Kluger & DeNisi, 1996	Goal difficulty	37	0.51	19
Walberg, 1999	General effects of setting goals or objectives	21	0.40	16
Burns, 2004[b]	Degree of challenge	45	0.82	29
Gollwitzer & Sheeran, 2006[b]	Goal intentions on achievement	94	0.72	26
Graham & Perin, 2007	Goal specificity	5	0.70	26

[a] Two effect sizes are listed because of the manner in which effect sizes were reported. Readers should consult the study for more details.

[b] As reported in Hattie (2009).

[c] Both Tubbs (1986) and Locke and Latham (1990) report results from organizational as well as educational settings.

[d] As reported in Locke and Latham (2002).

[e] The review includes a wide variety of ways and contexts in which goals might be used.

A scrutiny of the studies reported in table 1.5 provides a number of useful generalizations about learning goals and, by extrapolation, about learning progressions. First, setting goals appears to have a notable effect on student achievement in its own right. This is evidenced by the substantial ESs reported in table 1.5 for the general effects of goal setting. For example, Kevin Wise and James Okey (1983) reported an ES of 1.37, Mark Lipsey and David Wilson (1993) reported an ES of 0.55, and Herbert Walberg (1999) reported an ES of 0.40. Second, specific goals have more of an impact than do general goals. Witness Mark Tubbs's (1986) ES of 0.50 associated with setting specific goals as opposed to general goals. Edwin Locke and Gary Latham (1990) reported ESs that range from 0.42 to 0.82 regarding specific versus general goals, and Steve Graham and Dolores Perin (2007) reported an ES of 0.70 (for translations of ESs into percentile gains, see appendix B). Third, goals must be at the right level of difficulty for maximum effect on student achievement. This is evidenced in the findings reported by Tubbs (1986), Anthony Mento, Robert Steel, and Ronald Karren (1987), Locke and Latham (1990), Kluger and DeNisi (1996), and Matthew Burns (2004). Specifically, goals must be challenging enough to interest students but not so difficult as to frustrate them (for a detailed discussion of learning goals, see Marzano, 2009).

The Imprecision of Assessments

One fact that must be kept in mind in any discussion of assessment—formative or otherwise—is that all assessments are imprecise to one degree or another. This is explicit in a fundamental equation of classical test theory that can be represented as follows:

Observed score = true score + error score

Marzano (2006) explained:

> This equation indicates that a student's observed score on an assessment (the final score assigned by the teacher) consists of two components— the student's true score and the student's error score. The student's true score is that which represents the student's true level of understanding or skill regarding the topic being measured. The error score is the part of an observed score that is due to factors other than the student's level understanding or skill. (pp. 36–37)

In technical terms, every score assigned to a student on every assessment probably contains some part that is error. To illustrate the consequences of error in the interpretation of assessment scores, consider table 1.6.

Table 1.6 Ranges of Possible "True Scores" for Differing Levels of Reliability

Reliability of Assessment	Score Student Receives on the Assessment	Lowest Possible True Score	Highest Possible True Score	Range
0.85	70	60	80	20
0.75	70	58	82	24
0.65	70	56	84	28
0.55	70	54	86	32
0.45	70	52	88	36

Note: 95% confidence interval based on the assumption of a standard deviation of 12 points.

Table 1.6 shows what can be expected in terms of the amount of error that surrounds a score of 70 when an assessment has reliabilities that range from 0.85 to 0.45. In all cases, the student is assumed to have received a score of 70 on the assessment. That is, the student's observed score is 70.

First, let us consider the precision of an observed score of 70 when the reliability of the assessment is 0.85. This is the typical reliability one would expect from a standardized test or a state test (Lou et al., 1996). Using statistical formulas, it is possible to compute a range of scores in which you are 95 percent sure the true score actually falls. Columns three, four, and five of table 1.6 report that range. In the first row of table 1.6, we see that for an assessment with a reliability of 0.85 and an observed score of 70, one would be 95 percent sure the student's true score is anywhere between a score of 60 and 80. That is, the student's true score might really be as low as 60 or as high as 80 even though he or she receives a score of 70. This is a range of 20 points. But this assumes the reliability of the assessment to be 0.85, which, again, is what you would expect from a state test or a standardized test.

Next, let us consider the range with classroom assessments. To do so, consider the second row of table 1.6, which pertains to the reliability of 0.75. This is probably the highest reliability you could expect from an assessment designed by a teacher, school, or district (see Lou et al., 1996). Now the low score is 58 and the high score is 82—a range of 24 points. To obtain the full impact of the information presented in table 1.6, consider the last row, which depicts the range of possible true scores when the reliability is 0.45. This reliability is, in fact, probably more typical of what you could expect from a teacher-designed classroom assessment (Marzano, 2002). The lowest possible true score is 52 and the highest possible true score is 88—a range of 36 points.

Quite obviously, no single assessment can ever be relied on as an absolute indicator of a student's status. Gregory Cizek (2007) added a perspective on the precision of assessments in his discussion on the mathematics section of the state test in a large midwestern state. He explained that the total score reliability for the mathematics portion of the test in that state at the fourth grade is 0.87—certainly an acceptable level of reliability. That test also reports students' scores in subareas using the National Council of Teachers of Mathematics categories: algebra, data analysis and probability, estimation and mental computation, geometry, and problem-solving strategies. Unfortunately, the reliability of these subscale scores ranges from 0.33 to 0.57 (p. 103). As evidenced by table 1.6, reliabilities this low would translate into a wide range of possible true scores.

Imprecision in assessments can come in many forms. It can be a function of poorly constructed items on a test, or it can come from students' lack of attention or effort when taking a test. Imprecision can also be a function of teachers' interpretations of assessments. A study done by Herman and Choi (2008) asked two questions: How accurate are teachers' judgments of student learning, and how does accuracy of teachers' judgments relate to student performance? They found that "the study results show that the more accurate teachers are in their knowledge of where students are, the more effective they may be in promoting subsequent subject learning" (p. 18). Unfortunately, they also found that "average accuracy was less than 50%" (p. 19). Margaret Heritage, Jinok Kim, Terry Vendlinski, and Joan Herman (2008) added that "inaccurate analyses or inappropriate inference about students' learning status can lead to errors in what the next instructional steps will be" (p. 1). They concluded that "using assessment information to plan subsequent instruction tends to be the most difficult task for teachers as compared to other tasks (for example, assessing student responses)" (p. 14).

One very important consideration when interpreting scores from assessments or making inferences about a student based on an assessment is the native language of the student. Christy Kim Boscardin, Barbara Jones, Claire Nishimura, Shannon Madsen, and Jae-Eun Park (2008) conducted a review of performance assessments administered in high school biology courses. They focused their review on English language learners, noting that "the language demand of content assessments may introduce construct-irrelevant components into the testing process for EL students" (p. 3). Specifically, they found that the students with a stronger grasp of the English language would perform better on the tests even though they might not have had any better understanding of the science content. The same concept holds true for standardized tests in content-specific areas. They noted that "the language demand of a content assessment is a potential threat to the validity of the assessment" (p. 3).

Grading

At the classroom level, any discussion of assessment ultimately ends up in a discussion of grading. As its title indicates, *Formative Assessment and Standards-Based Grading* focuses on grading as well as on formative assessment. Not only are teachers responsible for evaluating a student's level of knowledge or skill at one point in time through classroom assessments, they are also responsible for translating all of the information from assessments into an overall evaluation of a student's performance over some fixed period of time (usually a quarter, trimester, or semester). This overall evaluation is in the form of some type of overall grade commonly referred to as an "omnibus grade." Unfortunately, grades add a whole new layer of error to the assessment process.

Brookhart (2004) discussed the difficulties associated with grading:

> Grades have been used to serve three general purposes simultaneously: ranking (for sorting students into those eligible for higher education and those not eligible); reporting results (accounting to parents the degree to which students learned the lessons prescribed for them); and contributing to learning (providing feedback and motivating students). (p. 23)

While all three purposes are valid, they provide very different perspectives on student achievement.

Since the teachers in many schools and districts have not agreed on any one grading philosophy, they are forced to design their own systems. To illustrate, consider the following grading criteria Thomas Guskey (2009, p. 17) listed as elements frequently included in teachers' grading practices:

- Major exams or compositions
- Class quizzes
- Reports or projects
- Student portfolios
- Exhibits of students' work
- Laboratory projects
- Students' notebooks or journals
- Classroom observations
- Oral presentations
- Homework completion
- Homework quality

- Class participation

- Work habits and neatness

- Effort

- Attendance

- Punctuality of assignments

- Class behavior or attitude

- Progress made

He made the point that because of their different philosophies, different teachers rely on different combinations of these elements to construct an overall grade. For example, one teacher might include major exams, quizzes, class participation, and punctuality of assignments in his or her grading policy while another teacher teaching exactly the same course might include major exams, reports, effort, and attendance. Consequently, the grading schemes for the same course taught by two different teachers might be so different that grades are not comparable from teacher to teacher. In effect, individual teachers' grades are interpretable only in the context of the grading scheme constructed by that specific teacher.

Norm-Referenced Grading

One approach to grading that has been used over the years is to report how students are performing in relation to one another. This might be called *norm-referenced grading*. In his doctoral dissertation, Kenneth Haponstall (2009) pointed out that this might have been the impetus for what was referred to as the "grading system" in the mid-nineteenth century, whereby students were grouped by level of knowledge and skill as well as by age so that teachers might provide more focused instruction to these homogeneous groups. He explained that James Baldwin (1884, in Haponstall, 2009) saw problems with the system even then, pointing out that no standard criteria about how students were "graded" or by whom had been established. The decision was subjective and left to anyone from the superintendent to the school secretary or a member of the board of education.

While few, if any, grading schemes currently in place use a strict norm-referenced approach, vestiges of it can be found in the practices of class rankings and grading on a curve.

Class Rankings

Class rankings are related to the concept of norm-referenced grading. Haponstall pointed out that "with districts using differing measures, including grade weighting for advanced placement classes, grade improvement for special education classes, [and] credit recovery for failed courses, there seems to be no standard method for schools to demonstrate those students who are showing academic excellence" (p. 22).

Lawrence Cross and Robert Frary (1999) noted that even though "grading is a hodgepodge of attitude, effort, and achievement at the middle and high school levels, colleges not only accept the grade point and class ranking in determining enrollment, but many are starting to use these measures exclusively" (as cited in Haponstall, 2009, p. 22). The admissions policies of many colleges exacerbate the practice of class ranking. To illustrate, David Lang (2007) pointed out that states such as California, Florida, and Texas guarantee a certain top percentage of each graduating class admission to a state school. This renders class ranks a high-stakes endeavor, particularly for those ranked too low for a guarantee of admission to a state school (as cited in Haponstall, 2009).

Grading on the Curve

When a teacher grades on the curve, he or she gives the highest grade to the student who performed best on an assessment and then gives every other student a grade by ranking his or her performance accordingly. This system essentially grades students in relation to one another. Thus, it has a basis in norm-referencing. Proponents for grading on the curve maintain that it is fair and equitable because most classes will have a normal distribution of achievement scores in any given subject area (for a discussion, see Brookhart, 2004).

Thomas Guskey (2009), however, maintained that "grading 'on the curve' communicates nothing about what students have learned or are able to do" (p. 11). Instead of telling teachers what a student has learned, it simply reports how much or how little he or she learned in relation to his or her fellow students. He also pointed to research by Benjamin Bloom (Bloom, 1976; Bloom, Madaus, & Hastings, 1981) indicating that student achievement does not necessarily follow a normal distribution when teachers exhibit a high level of instructional acumen. Grading students only in relation to one another, therefore, may provide information about a student's rank in class, but it does not speak to the student's academic achievement.

Self-Referenced Grading

Self-referenced grading occurs in relation to one's own past performances. Proponents say that it may reduce competition in classrooms and serve to motivate students (for a discussion, see Brookhart & Nitko, 2007). On first glance, this kind of grading seems to make intuitive sense: the reference point for each student is his or her personal growth and the extent of active engagement in his or her own learning. But Brookhart and Nitko pointed out that this form of grading tends to be used primarily with low-ability students, and while heavily weighting factors such as effort, behavior, attitude, and participation might seem positive, this emphasis is one of the major criticisms of this form of grading. Mixing nonacademic competencies with academic competencies contaminates the meaning of a grade.

Standards-Based Grading

Grading that references student achievement to specific topics within each subject area is growing in popularity. This is called standards-based grading, and many consider this method to be the most appropriate method of grading (for a discussion, see Brookhart & Nitko, 2007, p. 219). Where there is interest in this system, however, there is also quite a bit of poor practice on top of considerable confusion about its defining characteristics.

As described in Marzano (2006), the origins of standards-based reporting can be traced to the concept of a performance standard. The term was popularized in a 1993 report commonly referred to as the Malcom Report in deference to Shirley M. Malcom, chair of the planning group. The report defined a "performance standard" as "how good is good enough" (National Education Goals Panel, 1993, pp. ii–iii). Since then, a popular practice has been to define student performance in terms of four categories: advanced, proficient, basic, and below basic. The scheme has its roots in the work of the National Assessment of Educational Progress. As Popham (2003) noted:

> Increasingly, U.S. educators are building performance standards along the lines of the descriptive categories used in the National Assessment of Educational Progress (NAEP), a test administered periodically under the auspices of the federal government. NAEP results permit students' performances in participating states to be compared. . . . Since 1990, NAEP results

have been described in four performance categories: *advanced, proficient, basic,* and *below basic.* Most of the 50 states now use those four categories or labels quite similar to them. (p. 39)

The actual practice of standards-based reporting requires the identification of what we have referred to as reporting topics or measurement topics (Marzano, 2006; Marzano & Haystead, 2008). For example, consider the following common measurement topics for language arts at the fourth grade:

Reading

Word recognition and vocabulary

Reading comprehension

Literary analysis

Writing

Spelling

Language mechanics and conventions

Research and technology

Evaluation and revision

Listening and Speaking

Listening comprehension

Analysis and evaluation of oral media

Speaking applications

Here, ten measurement topics are organized under three categories (or strands, as some districts call them): reading, writing, and listening and speaking. For reporting purposes, each student would receive a score of advanced, proficient, basic, or below basic on each of the ten measurement topics. Typically, some type of rubric or scale that describes these levels is constructed for each measurement topic (we discuss this in depth in chapters 3, 5, and 6).

While this system seems like good practice, without giving teachers guidance and support on how to collect and interpret the assessment data with which scores like advanced, proficient, basic, and below basic are assigned, standards-based reporting can be highly inaccurate. Indeed, at the writing of this book, no major study (that we are aware of) has demonstrated that simply grading in a standards-based manner enhances student achievement. However, as the previous discussion illustrates, a fairly strong case can be made that student achievement will be positively affected if standards-based reporting is rooted in a clear-cut system of formative assessments.

Another problem that plagues standards-based reporting is the lack of distinction between *standards-referenced* systems and *standards-based* systems. Grant Wiggins (1993, 1996) was perhaps the first modern-day educator to highlight the differences between a standards-based system and a standards-referenced system. In a standards-based system, a student does not move to the next level until he or she can demonstrate competence at the current level. In a standards-referenced system, a student's status is reported (or referenced) relative to the performance standard for each area of knowledge and skill on the report card; however, even if the student does not meet the performance standard for each topic, he or she moves to the next level. Thus, the vast majority of schools and districts that claim to have standards-based systems in fact have standards-referenced systems. As we shall see in chapter 6, both systems are viable, but they are quite different in their underlying philosophies. Understanding the distinctions between standards-based and standards-referenced systems helps schools and districts design a grading system that meets their needs.

Translating Research Into Classroom Practice

In subsequent chapters, we draw from the research and theory in this chapter and from sources such as *Classroom Assessment and Grading That Work* (Marzano, 2006) and *Designing and Teaching Learning Goals and Objectives* (Marzano, 2009) to discuss how formative assessment can be effectively implemented in the classroom. We also outline a system of grading that, when used uniformly and consistently, can yield much more valid and reliable information than that provided by traditional grading systems.

As mentioned in the introduction, as you progress through the remaining chapters, you will encounter exercises that ask you to examine the content presented. Some of these exercises ask you to answer specific questions. Answer these questions and check your answers with those provided in the back of the book. Other exercises are more open-ended and ask you to generate applications of what you have read.

Chapter 2

THE ANATOMY OF FORMATIVE ASSESSMENT

The discussion in chapter 1 highlights both the interest in and the confusion about formative assessment and its use in K–12 classrooms. An obvious question one might ask is, Why the confusion? To answer this question, it is useful to understand some history about the term *formative assessment*. Initially, it was used in the field of evaluation. In an American Educational Research Association monograph series published in 1967, Michael Scriven pointed out the distinction between evaluating projects that were being formulated and evaluating those that had evolved to their final state. The former were referred to as formative evaluations and the latter were referred to as summative evaluations.

In the world of projects, the distinction between formative evaluation and summative evaluation makes perfect sense. Consider a project in which a new curriculum for elementary school mathematics is being developed. There is a clear beginning point at which the authors of the program start putting their ideas on paper. There are benchmarks along the way, such as completing a first draft, gathering feedback on that draft, and making revisions based on the feedback. Finally, there is a clear ending point when the new curriculum has been published and is being distributed to schools.

According to Popham (2008), Benjamin Bloom tried in 1969 to transplant the formative/summative evaluation distinction directly into assessment, but "few educators were interested in investigating this idea further because it seemed to possess few practical implications for the day-to-day world of schooling" (p. 4). As described in chapter 1, it would take until the Black and Wiliam (1998a) synthesis for the idea to catch on. At that time, they offered the following definition of formative assessment:

> Formative assessment . . . is to be interpreted as all of those activities undertaken by teachers and/or by students which provide information to be used as feedback to modify the teaching and learning activities in which they engage. (pp. 7–8)

In 2006, the Council of Chief State School Officers (CCSSO) attempted to tighten the definition of formative assessments. According to Popham (2008),

> A central activity in the CCSSO assessment initiative was the creation of a new consortium focused specifically on formative assessment. A CCSSO consortium is composed of key department of education personnel from

those states that wish to participate. Each of these groups is referred to as a State Collaborative on Assessment and Student Standards (SCASS), and a new SCASS dealing exclusively with formative assessment, known as Formative Assessment for Students and Teachers—or FAST SCASS, if you're in a hurry—was formed in mid-2006. (pp. 4–5)

At its inaugural four-day meeting in October of 2006, FAST SCASS crafted a definition of formative assessment that reflected the latest research on effective assessment practices. As reported by Popham, the following definition came out of this effort: "Formative assessment is a process used by teachers and students during instruction that provides feedback to adjust ongoing teaching and learning to improve students' achievement of intended instructional outcomes" (2008, p. 5). Defining features of formative assessment were as follows:

- Formative assessment is a *process*, not any particular test.

- It is used not just by teachers but by *both teachers and students*.

- Formative assessment takes place *during* instruction.

- It provides *assessment-based feedback* to teachers and students.

- The function of this feedback is to help teachers and students make *adjustments* that will improve students' achievement of intended curricular aims. (Popham, 2008, p. 5)

In his 2008 book *Transformative Assessment*, Popham updated that definition again: "Formative assessment is a planned process in which teachers or students use assessment-based evidence to adjust what they are currently doing" (p. 6). He also listed the following characteristics:

- Again, formative assessment is not a test but a process—a *planned* process involving a number of different activities.

- One of those activities is the use of assessments, both formal and informal, to elicit *evidence regarding students' status*: the degree to which a particular student has mastered a particular skill or body of knowledge.

- Based on this evidence, *teachers adjust* their ongoing instructional activities or *students adjust* the procedures they're currently using to try to learn whatever they're trying to learn. (p. 6)

The preceding definitions have certainly illustrated the general concept of formative assessment, but this book is intended to go one step further by specifying how formative assessment might manifest in the classroom. To this end, the categories depicted in table 2.1 are used throughout the book. Table 2.1 addresses two important distinctions in classroom assessment: types of assessments and uses of assessments. This chapter attempts to flesh out the defining characteristics of both.

Before delving into the anatomy of formative assessment, we should begin with a working definition of classroom assessment in general. Paraphrasing from the distinctions made in *Classroom Assessment and Grading That Work* (Marzano, 2006), we will define a classroom assessment as anything a teacher does to gather information about a student's knowledge or skill regarding a specific topic. This definition is very much in keeping with the general descriptions of assessment provided by Black and Wiliam in their 1998 article titled "Inside the Black Box: Raising Standards Through Classroom Assessment."

That work was a brief description of the findings from their synthesis of 250 studies on formative assessment. They noted:

> We use the general term *assessment* to refer to all those activities undertaken by teachers—and by their students in assessing themselves—that provide information to be used as feedback to modify teaching and learning activities. (1998b, p. 2)

Interestingly, this definition is almost identical to the definition of formative assessment they offered in their more technical discussion of their findings, "Assessment and Classroom Learning," which was also published in 1998. As stated previously, their definition of formative assessment was:

> Formative assessment . . . is to be interpreted as all of those activities undertaken by teachers and/or by their students which provide information to be used as feedback to modify the teaching and learning activities in which they are engaged. (1998a, pp. 7–8)

The similarities in definitions for the general construct of assessment and the more specific construct of formative assessment highlight the need for clearer distinctions. Examining types of assessment in contrast to uses of assessment helps provide these distinctions.

Types of Classroom Assessments

According to table 2.1, there are three types of assessments a teacher might use in the classroom: obtrusive assessments, unobtrusive assessments, and student-generated assessments. Each can and should be used in a comprehensive system of formative assessment.

Table 2.1 Distinctions Regarding Classroom Assessments

Types of Classroom Assessment
Obtrusive
Unobtrusive
Student generated
Uses of Classroom Assessment
Formative scores
Summative scores
Instructional feedback

Obtrusive Assessments

Obtrusive assessments interrupt the normal flow of activity in the classroom. Instruction does not occur during obtrusive assessments. Instead, instruction stops while students "take the assessment" (hence the term *obtrusive*).

Obtrusive assessments can take many forms. Probably the most common form is the paper/pencil test. For example, as a form of obtrusive assessment, a science teacher schedules a quiz to assess students' understanding of the concept of mutualism, or a language arts teacher provides a five-item short-answer test designed to assess the students' comprehension of a reading passage.

Demonstrations and performances can also be forms of obtrusive assessments. For example, as a form of obtrusive assessment, a dance teacher asks students to perform a dance step they have been practicing during the week, a physical education teacher focusing on basketball asks students to demonstrate the proper execution of a free throw, or a science teacher asks students to demonstrate how the cell membrane is selectively permeable by designing and explaining a model. Obtrusive assessments can also be oral. For example, as a form of obtrusive assessment, a social studies teacher asks an individual student to explain the defining characteristics of a constitutional democracy. In all of these examples, instruction stops while assessment occurs. The following examples depict obtrusive assessments in a variety of subject areas.

Language arts: To assess the students' ability to write a persuasive paper, the teacher assigns students the task of identifying a claim about a topic of their choice and supporting that claim with appropriate facts and qualifiers. Students begin the task in class and turn it in the next day.

Mathematics: To assess the students' ability to make reasonable estimations of weight, students are given four objects each. They must consider the weight of each object and write down estimations they consider to be reasonable using the units of measure studied in class. They must also write brief justifications for their answers. At the end of class, the students turn in their assessments.

Science: To assess the students' understanding of the systems of the human body, the teacher provides them with a blank outline of a human body. He asks them to graphically locate the heart, the lungs, the liver, and the stomach. They are also asked to write down the system associated with each organ and provide brief explanations of that system's major purpose.

Social studies: To assess the students' knowledge of United States geography, the teacher provides a blank map of the country. Students must write in the names of as many states as they can in the time allotted.

Physical education: To assess the students' ability to hit a golf ball, the teacher asks each student to demonstrate a golf swing using a driver. After hitting the ball, each student is asked to evaluate his or her own swing and name one thing he or she could have done to make it better. After analyzing the swing, the student is asked to demonstrate again, this time thinking in advance about what he or she needs to improve on.

Art: To assess the students' ability to draw using perspective, the teacher presents them with three-dimensional objects such as cylinders, prisms, and cubes. They are asked to choose one object and use the relevant elements of perspective to draw it as realistically as possible within the allotted time.

Technology: To assess the students' ability to use PowerPoint, the teacher assigns students the task of creating a brief PowerPoint presentation designed to teach their classmates about one of their hobbies. Students begin the task in class and are asked to finish the projects at home in preparation for in-class presentations the next day.

Unobtrusive Assessments

In contrast to obtrusive assessments, unobtrusive assessments do not interrupt the flow of instruction. In fact, students might not even be aware that they are being assessed during an unobtrusive assessment.

Unobtrusive assessments are most easily applied to content that is procedural, or content that involves learning a skill, strategy, or process. For example, a physical education teacher observes a student on the playground executing an overhand throw and notes that he or she performs the skill quite well; during independent work in the laboratory, a science teacher notes that a particular student is not following the correct procedure for combining chemicals safely. Each of these situations provides the teacher with information about the student's current status regarding a specific skill, strategy, or process, but in neither case is the student aware that such information has been obtained by the teacher. The following examples briefly depict unobtrusive assessments that might be employed in various subject areas.

Language arts: A teacher observes a student writing a haiku poem of his or her own design. The teacher considers this an unobtrusive assessment of the student's ability to write this type of poem.

Mathematics: A teacher observes a student working a division problem from a homework assignment on the board. The student works through the problem correctly, and the teacher considers this an unobtrusive assessment of the student's ability to perform the process of division.

Science: A teacher observes a student performing the steps of a scientific procedure and taking notes in a lab book. The teacher considers this an unobtrusive assessment of the student's ability to perform and document a scientific experiment.

Social studies: A teacher observes a student identifying on a map of the city where his or her house is located. The teacher considers this an unobtrusive assessment of the student's ability to read a map.

Physical education: A teacher observes a student stopping a soccer ball with his or her feet and then kicking it to a teammate during a game played in class. The teacher considers this an unobtrusive assessment of the student's ability to stop a ball and kick it with accuracy.

Art: A teacher observes a student acting a part in a role-playing exercise and considers this an unobtrusive assessment of the student's ability to create and maintain a character.

Technology: A teacher observes a student typing with correct technique while looking at the computer screen instead of the keyboard. He or she considers this an unobtrusive assessment of the student's typing ability.

Student-Generated Assessments

Student-generated assessments are probably the most underutilized form of classroom assessment. As the name implies, a defining feature of student-generated assessments is that students generate ideas about the manner in which they will demonstrate their current status on a given topic. To do so, they might use any of the types of obtrusive assessments discussed in the preceding text. For example, one student might say that she will provide an oral answer to any of the twenty questions in the back of chapter 3 of the science textbook to demonstrate her knowledge of the topic of habitats. Another student might propose that he design and explain a model of the cell membrane to demonstrate his knowledge of the topic. The following examples depict student-generated assessments that might be employed in various subject areas.

Language arts: To demonstrate her understanding of a book read in class, a fifth-grade student proposes that she write a paper describing the events of the story and how one event caused another, leading to the story's ultimate resolution.

Mathematics: To demonstrate his understanding of geometric angles, a fourth-grade student proposes that he measure and draw acute, obtuse, and right angles as well as complementary and supplementary angles in the presence of the teacher.

Science: To show that she understands the solar system, an eighth-grade student proposes that she draw a diagram of the solar system and write a paper describing the major features of each different planet and its relationship to the other planets in the system.

Social studies: To demonstrate his understanding of the causes of World War II, an eighth-grade student proposes that he write a paper on how the war might have been avoided if the Treaty of Versailles had not been so punitive to Germany.

Physical education: To show that she can do a forward and a backward roll, a kindergarten student offers to demonstrate both movements for the teacher.

Art: To show his skill at shading, a sixth-grade student offers to draw and shade an object in his house and bring the drawing to class.

Technology: To show that she understands how email works, a first-grade student offers to send the teacher an email from the school computer lab and bring a printed copy of the teacher's reply to class.

Exercise 2.1 provides some practice in classifying assessments. (See page 35 for a reproducible of this exercise and page 132 for a reproducible answer sheet. Visit **marzanoresearch.com/classroom strategiesthatwork** to download all the exercises and answers in this book.)

Exercise 2.1
Obtrusive, Unobtrusive, and Student-Generated Assessments

After reading each of the following classroom assessment scenarios, determine whether it is best classified as an example of obtrusive, unobtrusive, or student-generated assessment.

1. Mona is very close to receiving an A on the content that has been covered in her art class this quarter. She approaches the teacher and proposes that she provide a sketch to show she has mastered the techniques presented during the quarter.

2. After teaching the concept of a thesis statement, discussing examples of successful thesis statements, and providing the students with opportunities for practice, Mr. Grace gives his students a topic and asks them to write a corresponding thesis statement. He scores the effectiveness of the thesis statements using a rubric and records the scores for each student.

3. After teaching a unit on editing and revising, Ms. Minturn asks her students to pull out a hard copy of an essay they composed earlier in the year. She breaks the class into pairs and asks them to read and suggest edits and revisions on their partners' essays. She collects the revisions and grades each student according to a rubric on the effectiveness of his or her editing.

4. Mr. Davis is teaching a unit on shading. He takes his class to an outside garden, and while the students are creating compositions focusing on the shadows and colors they see, he walks around and observes their progress. Without interrupting, he records an assessment score for each student in his gradebook.

5. Ms. Lewis has been working with her students on a cooperative learning goal. While she is monitoring recess, she notices four of them working together to complete a double-dutch jump rope game. Because all four students have to cooperate to reach their goal, Ms. Lewis decides these students have fulfilled the requirement for score 3.0 on the rubric she has designed for cooperative skills.

Uses of Classroom Assessments

As depicted in table 2.1 (page 23), there are three different uses of classroom assessments: formative scores, summative scores, and instructional feedback.

Formative and Summative Scores

As described in the first part of this chapter, the formal definition of formative assessment and Popham's (2008) amendments to that definition indicate that formative assessment is a process as opposed to a specific type of assessment. In fact, it would be accurate to say that, in general, a specific assessment is neither formative nor summative—it all depends on how the information is used. Theoretically then, the same assessment could be used in a formative sense or in a summative sense. John Hattie (2003) made this point quite eloquently:

> As illustrated by Bob Stake's maxim: when the cook tastes the soup it is formative, when the guests taste the soup it is summative. Thus a key issue is timing, and it is possible that the same stimulus (e.g., tasting the soup) can be interpreted and used for both forms of assessment. Hence, it is NOT the instrument . . . that is formative and summative. It is the timing of the interpretation and the purpose to which the information is used. (p. 4)

This noted, it is also true that assessments can and perhaps should be tailored to collect data that will be used for either formative purposes or summative purposes but not both. As noted by Pellegrino, Chudowsky, and Glaser (2001): "Often a single assessment is used for multiple purposes; in general however, the more purposes a single assessment aims to serve, the more each purpose will be compromised" (p. 2).

For the reasons cited in the preceding text, throughout this work, the terms *formative scores* and *summative scores* are used in lieu of the terms formative assessment and summative assessment. Assessments, then, can have multiple forms (obtrusive, unobtrusive, and student generated) and multiple uses, two of which are to generate formative scores and summative scores. This focus on formative and summative scores as opposed to formative and summative assessments provides a unique perspective on classroom assessment and tracking students' progress over time. To illustrate, consider figure 2.1 (page 28).

In figure 2.1, four formative scores have been assigned to the student, Lindsay, on the topic of writing transitions in expository compositions. Each of these scores is on a scale from 0 through 4, indicating that the teacher used a rubric to score this particular skill. Each score represents the student's level of knowledge at a certain point in time. The last (fourth) score in the sequence is not necessarily the summative score. The summative score (recorded to the far right of the graph in the last column, labeled "S") represents the teacher's judgment about Lindsay's final status based on all of the previous scores. To illustrate how a summative score is generated, consider figure 2.2 (page 29).

The depiction in figure 2.2 is certainly different from traditional approaches to keeping track of students' scores. It is also different from the recommendation of some authors that formative scores should not be recorded since they are to be used only as practice for summative assessments. In this book, we take strong exception to that perspective for one major reason: *a summative score should not be derived from a single final assessment.* Rather, a summative score should be the most reasonable representation of a student's final status at a particular point in time. All available information about a student should be used in the determination of his or her final status—his or her summative score. This practice is quite consistent with the sentiment of the members of the Committee on the Foundations of Assessment, who produced the ground-breaking book in assessment titled *Knowing What Students Know*: "The committee recognizes that all assessments are in a sense 'formative'" (Pellegrino et al., 2001, p. 38).

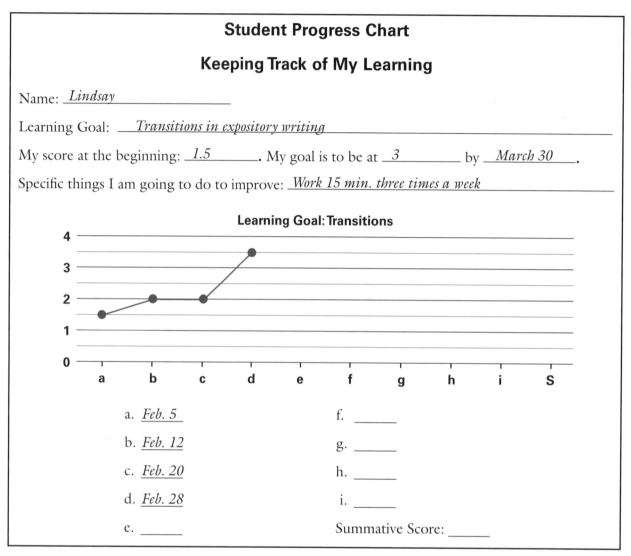

Student Progress Chart

Keeping Track of My Learning

Name: *Lindsay*

Learning Goal: *Transitions in expository writing*

My score at the beginning: *1.5*. My goal is to be at *3* by *March 30*.

Specific things I am going to do to improve: *Work 15 min. three times a week*

Learning Goal: Transitions

a. *Feb. 5*		f. _____
b. *Feb. 12*		g. _____
c. *Feb. 20*		h. _____
d. *Feb. 28*		i. _____
e. _____		Summative Score: _____

Figure 2.1 Line graph depicting formative scores.

To construct a summative score, the teacher examines the student's pattern of responses over time. *The teacher does not compute an average of the student's formative scores to construct a summative score.* This would be an absolute violation of the principles of formative assessment. The technical reason averaging makes little sense is explained in some depth in *Classroom Assessment and Grading That Work* (Marzano, 2006). The short version of that explanation is that averaging makes sense only if no learning has occurred from assessment to assessment or if assessments measure very different things. Obviously, in a formative system, all assessments for a particular topic will be on the same topic. This is the case in figures 2.1 and 2.2—all four assessments pertain to the student's (Lindsay's) skill at writing paragraphs with good transitions. As depicted in figures 2.1 and 2.2, Lindsay's first formative score was a 1.5, and her last was a 3.5. The average of these four formative scores (1.5, 2.0, 2.0, and 3.5) is 2.25, which certainly does not reflect her status at the end of the grading period.

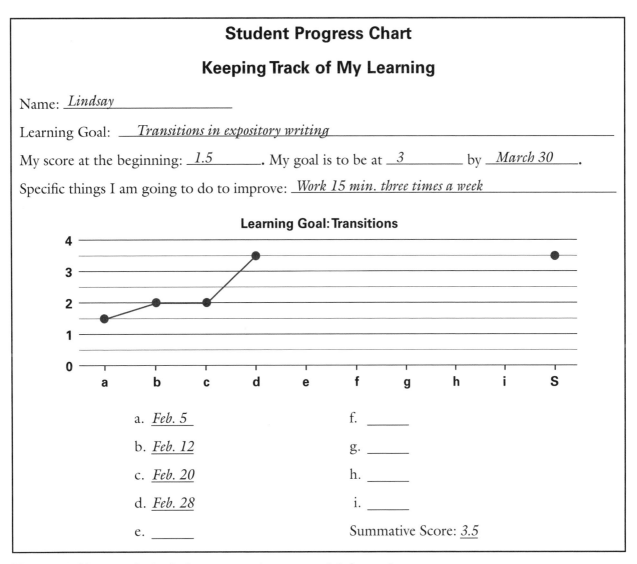

Figure 2.2 Line graph depicting summative score with formative scores.

A logical question some educators ask is, Why not simply use the student's final score as the summative score? The answer to this question was provided in chapter 1 in the discussion of error found in all assessments (see table 1.6, page 13). Recall that all assessments contain error, and one has to take that error into consideration when interpreting any single score as an estimation of a student's true status (or true score) at any point in time. Thus, the final formative score in a series of formative scores might, in fact, be an accurate indicator of a student's true score at that time, but it might not be.

A second question asked by educators (which is related to the first) is, Why not administer a final assessment and consider this as the summative score? The answer to this question is the same as the answer to the first question. Even if a very good final assessment is designed, it will still contain error. Consequently, it cannot be absolutely trusted as the true score for an individual student. This noted, it is still a viable and useful (but not absolutely necessary) practice for teachers to design some type of final examination and then enter that score into the mix with other formative scores. Obviously, the formative score that is based on a detailed final examination would receive more weight in determining a summative score than would previous formative scores.

To consolidate the discussion thus far, it is useful to list the characteristics of formative scores as described in this book.

1. Formative scores can be derived from a variety of types of assessment that include obtrusive assessments, unobtrusive assessments, and student-generated assessments.

   The four formative scores depicted in figures 2.1 and 2.2 (pages 28 and 29) could have been generated by any of the three types of assessments. To illustrate, the first assessment for Lindsay might have been an essay designed by the teacher—an obtrusive assessment. The second assessment in figures 2.1 and 2.2 could have been unobtrusive in that the teacher happened to notice Lindsay's use of transition sentences in a composition done for another class. The third assessment might have been student generated in that Lindsay proposed to the teacher that she complete some structured exercises on the use of transitional sentences in a grammar and composition text. The fourth assessment could have been another obtrusive assessment, perhaps a second composition assigned by the teacher.

2. Assessments that yield formative scores must be scored.

   As we shall see in the next section, on instructional feedback, all assessments do not have to be scored. However, assessments must be scored if they are to be used to generate formative scores. Additionally, they must be recorded in some way, as depicted in figures 2.1 and 2.2.

3. A set of recorded formative scores is used to track student progress over time.

   As depicted in figures 2.1 and 2.2, formative scores should be recorded and displayed in such a way as to track student progress. In subsequent chapters, we will consider a variety of ways to display student progress, including technology-based approaches.

4. A set of formative scores is used to generate a summative score at the end of a particular interval of time, such as a grading period.

   One of the primary uses of formative scores is to generate a summative score. This is not done by averaging formative scores or simply using the last formative score in the set. As we shall see in chapters 5 and 6, formative scores can also be used to examine knowledge gain.

Instructional Feedback to Teachers and Students

In contrast to formative scores is instructional feedback. Table 2.2 depicts the similarities and differences between these uses of assessment.

As indicated in table 2.2, assessments used to generate formative and summative scores and assessments used for instructional feedback have common characteristics: both can involve obtrusive assessment, unobtrusive assessment, and student-generated assessment. Additionally, both can be scored, though scoring assessments used for instructional feedback is not required.

Table 2.2 Formative and Summative Scores Versus Instructional Feedback

Formative and Summative Scores	Instructional Feedback
Formative and summative scores can be derived from a variety of types of assessments that include obtrusive assessments, unobtrusive assessments, and student-generated assessments.	Instructional feedback can be derived from a variety of types of assessments that include obtrusive assessments, unobtrusive assessments, and student-generated assessments.
Assessments are scored.	Assessments may or may not be scored.
Scores are recorded and used to track student progress.	Because assessments are not recorded, they are not part of the formative tracking of students over time, but they do serve to inform the teacher about how both the class and specific students are progressing.
Formative scores are used to generate a summative score.	Instructional feedback is not a formal part of the design of summative scores, but it may help teachers determine the most appropriate summative score for specific students.

To illustrate how instructional feedback might manifest in the classroom, consider the following examples:

- In response to questions the teacher asks, students hold their thumbs up to signal they know the answer, hold their thumbs down to signal they do not know the answer, and hold their thumbs to the side to signal they are not sure if they know the answer.

- A teacher gives a practice quiz that is scored on the spot by students as the teacher goes through the answers. Each student scores his or her own answers. As the teacher goes over each question, he or she asks students to raise their hands if they feel they need more help with the content. At the end of the activity, each student knows how he or she scored on the practice test, and the teacher has a sense of how well the class did.

- After students have practiced strategies for the overhand throw of a softball, a teacher observes them at recess playing a game of softball. He mentally makes a note of how well each student is executing the throw and uses this feedback to help redesign the next lesson with students. In class, he provides feedback to specific students based on what he saw at recess.

Note that each of the activities qualifies as an assessment in that it provides information about students' level of knowledge or skill regarding a specific topic. In the first example, the assessment involves questions posed by the teacher orally. All students respond to the questions using hand signals. This is a form of obtrusive assessment. Because it is oral and because the whole class responds to every question, student responses are not scored.

In the second example, the form of assessment is more formal—the teacher gives a quiz. Additionally, the quiz is scored. Right after the quiz, the teacher goes over each item as students score their own papers. As before, this is an obtrusive assessment, but this time individual student scores are generated. However, because the assessment is designed for instructional feedback, students' scores are not recorded.

The third example is an unobtrusive form of assessment. The teacher observes students executing a physical skill and makes mental notes. The teacher does not assign scores. Instead, he uses the observations to redesign the next lesson and identify the feedback he wants to provide to specific students.

In addition to the characteristics in the preceding list, instructional feedback typically involves a great deal of interaction between teacher and students. In the first example, this might manifest as the teacher asking students why they think certain answers are correct or incorrect. The same is true for the second example. As the teacher goes over the answers with students to the various questions in the quiz, he or she might engage students in a dialogue about the strength of specific answers. In the third example, the teacher might have an extended conversation with students about their individual techniques, inviting input from them about ways to improve. In effect, instructional feedback provides an opportunity for teachers and students to reexamine content with the added benefit of assessment data that provide an indication of their current status.

In some cases, assessments used for instructional feedback are employed serially within a single lesson. Consider again the example in which the teacher asks questions orally and students respond using hand signals. The teacher might begin the class with a series of such questions, many of which the majority of students answer incorrectly. After some input from the teacher, another set of similar questions might be posed. More, but not all, students might respond favorably. Again, input is provided to students, and a third and final set of related questions is asked—this time with all of the students answering the questions correctly. In this approach, assessments used for instructional feedback are scaffolds that gradually increase the knowledge level of the class as a whole.

Exercise 2.2 provides some practice in discerning between instructional feedback and formative scores. (See page 36 for a reproducible of this exercise and page 134 for a reproducible answer sheet. Visit **marzanoresearch.com/classroomstrategiesthatwork** to download all the exercises and answers in this book.)

Exercise 2.2
Instructional Feedback Versus Formative Scores

After reading each of the following classroom scenarios, determine whether it illustrates an assessment being used for instructional feedback or for formative scores.

1. Ms. Levine is teaching a unit on oral communication. At the end of the unit, students will give an oral presentation on a book of their choosing, but Ms. Levine knows students need opportunities to practice skills such as eye contact, enunciation, and pace and volume control. To provide those opportunities, Ms. Levine asks the students more direct questions than she ordinarily might. The student who answers is asked to stand and address the class so that he or she may become a bit more comfortable with speaking in front of a group. Ms. Levine provides spontaneous feedback as well, such as suggesting that a student slow down or speak louder.

2. After a unit on the circulatory system, Mr. Williams asks students to complete a written test. He grades each one and records the scores.

3. Ms. Bowman has given her students updates on their current scores for each learning goal covered during the first quarter of the school year. Candice has been reminded that her score for a goal involving immigration is 2.5 on a 4-point rubric, and she wants to raise that score to 3.0 by the end of the quarter. She approaches Ms. Bowman with an idea to create a family tree depicting the names of each family member on her mother's side, the countries from which they came, and the date of their arrival. Candice believes this would demonstrate her knowledge of the score 3.0 content.

4. Mr. McKimm is teaching a unit on quadratic equations. He writes an equation and its solution on the blackboard and asks the class to vote on whether the solution is correct or incorrect. He chooses one student to explain why he or she thinks the solution is correct and one to explain why he or she thinks the solution is incorrect. After hearing both sides, the students vote again. Mr. McKimm makes a mental note of how many students appear to understand the problem.

5. Ms. Walker is teaching a unit on volleyball. After covering individual skills with the students, she has split them up into teams. During one of the games, she notices that Ashley executes a perfect overhand serve. Ashley has had trouble with this skill, receiving low scores in the past. After seeing the serve, Ms. Walker makes a mental note to assign Ashley a higher score in the gradebook.

The Importance of Changing Behavior

One of the defining features of the process of formative assessment as described in this book is that it provides information to students and teachers regarding adaptations they might make to improve performances. On the students' side, this involves identifying the specific content they must improve on and things they might do to improve. For example, after receiving instructional feedback on her use of the overhand throw, a student realizes that she needs to hold the softball looser when she throws. She decides to try this the next time she is in gym class.

On the teacher's side, behavior change involves identifying content that must be reviewed or retaught. For example, after scoring the practice quiz with students, the teacher realizes that he needs to review some vocabulary about the topic that he thought students already knew. The following scenarios provide examples of how the process of formative assessment can be used by teachers and students to adapt their behaviors in the service of learning.

Scenario 1: Ms. Butler is a high school language arts teacher who has just given an obtrusive assessment and is now recording the scores for formative purposes. She notices that almost all of the students performed poorly on an essay asking them to discuss the significance of the Arctic climate in the book *Frankenstein*. She realizes that while the class had discussed other, more concrete symbols in the book, they had not once during the school year touched on the ways setting can be used as a symbol. She decides to revisit this essay with the class and discuss the wide range of symbolic possibilities in any novel, using the Arctic climate in *Frankenstein* as an example.

Scenario 2: Mr. Mercer is an elementary art teacher who is unobtrusively assessing his students while they make origami holiday ornaments. He notices that while students seem to be doing well constructing the ornaments from precut pieces of paper, they are having a hard time cutting any pieces on their own. He realizes that while he went over in detail the processes of folding and constructing the ornaments, he did so with paper he had prepared by precutting. He decides to interrupt the class activity and go over the procedures for cutting so that students can perform the learning goal with more proficiency.

Scenario 3: The teacher has just given Maeve her score on the last quiz she took. She notices that she missed both items on soil salinization. Also, the teacher wrote on her paper, "Maeve, you seem to be confused about this." Maeve immediately goes to the Internet to try to determine where she is inaccurate.

Scenario 4: Mr. Cumberbund is a middle school social studies teacher who has just given an obtrusive assessment for formative purposes on the topic of government. He notices that while students performed well on questions regarding the executive and legislative branches of the government, almost all of them performed poorly on questions relating to the judicial branch. When rethinking his teaching strategies, he realizes that the content he covered had more to do with specific influential rulings of the Supreme Court and not the workings and purposes of the judicial branch in general. He decides to revisit this topic using a different approach.

Scenario 5: Aida has just participated in an activity in which students in her class were asked to vote on which answers they thought were correct for a series of questions on primary sources. For the first time, she realizes that she is very confused about this concept and resolves to ask her teacher about it as soon as she gets the chance.

Exercise 2.3 provides review questions for this chapter. (See page 37 for a reproducible of this exercise and page 136 for a reproducible answer sheet. Visit **marzanoresearch.com/classroomstrat egiesthatwork** to download all the exercises and answers in this book.)

Exercise 2.3
Review Questions

The following questions deal with much of the important content in this chapter. Answer each one and then compare your answers with those provided on the corresponding answer sheet.

1. What are the three types of classroom assessment, and what are some of the unique qualities of each?

2. What are the three ways to use assessments, and what are some of the unique characteristics of each?

3. What is the difference between formative assessment and formative scores as defined in *Formative Assessment and Standards-Based Grading*?

4. Describe how assessments can provide information to teachers about their own performances.

Summary

This chapter began with defining assessment as a broad construct involving anything that is done to provide information about students' knowledge and skill regarding content for a particular topic in class. Formative assessment is defined as a process that narrows the scope by requiring that the assessments be used for purposes of modification. There are three types of classroom assessment: obtrusive assessment, unobtrusive assessment, and student-generated assessment. Obtrusive is the most traditional form, and it involves interrupting instruction to "take" the assessment. Unobtrusive assessments can be employed informally for individual students whenever a teacher witnesses a student performing a relevant skill, strategy, or process. Student-generated assessments are those the students design and execute under the guidance of a teacher to improve a score or grade. Each of these types can be used in three ways: to create formative scores, or scores that are recorded in the interest of providing information to students and teachers about the progression of learning; to create summative scores, or scores that are derived at the end of a grading period and represent a student's final status at a particular point in time; or to provide instructional feedback, in which case assessments may be scored but are not recorded and are used to help inform students about areas of improvement and teachers about the progression of individual students or an entire class.

Exercise 2.1

Obtrusive, Unobtrusive, and Student-Generated Assessments

After reading each of the following classroom assessment scenarios, determine whether it is best classified as an example of obtrusive, unobtrusive, or student-generated assessment.

1. Mona is very close to receiving an A on the content that has been covered in her art class this quarter. She approaches the teacher and proposes that she provide a sketch to show she has mastered the techniques presented during the quarter.

2. After teaching the concept of a thesis statement, discussing examples of successful thesis statements, and providing the students with opportunities for practice, Mr. Grace gives his students a topic and asks them to write a corresponding thesis statement. He scores the effectiveness of the thesis statements using a rubric and records the scores for each student.

3. After teaching a unit on editing and revising, Ms. Minturn asks her students to pull out a hard copy of an essay they composed earlier in the year. She breaks the class into pairs and asks them to read and suggest edits and revisions on their partners' essays. She collects the revisions and grades each student according to a rubric on the effectiveness of his or her editing.

4. Mr. Davis is teaching a unit on shading. He takes his class to an outside garden, and while the students are creating compositions focusing on the shadows and colors they see, he walks around and observes their progress. Without interrupting, he records an assessment score for each student in his gradebook.

5. Ms. Lewis has been working with her students on a cooperative learning goal. While she is monitoring recess, she notices four of them working together to complete a double-dutch jump rope game. Because all four students have to cooperate to reach their goal, Ms. Lewis decides these students have fulfilled the requirement for score 3.0 on the rubric she has designed for cooperative skills.

Exercise 2.2

Instructional Feedback Versus Formative Scores

After reading each of the following classroom scenarios, determine whether it illustrates an assessment being used for instructional feedback or for formative scores.

1. Ms. Levine is teaching a unit on oral communication. At the end of the unit, students will give an oral presentation on a book of their choosing, but Ms. Levine knows students need opportunities to practice skills such as eye contact, enunciation, and pace and volume control. To provide those opportunities, Ms. Levine asks the students more direct questions than she ordinarily might. The student who answers is asked to stand and address the class so that he or she may become a bit more comfortable with speaking in front of a group. Ms. Levine provides spontaneous feedback as well, such as suggesting that a student slow down or speak louder.

2. After a unit on the circulatory system, Mr. Williams asks students to complete a written test. He grades each one and records the scores.

3. Ms. Bowman has given her students updates on their current scores for each learning goal covered during the first quarter of the school year. Candice has been reminded that her score for a goal involving immigration is 2.5 on a 4-point rubric, and she wants to raise that score to 3.0 by the end of the quarter. She approaches Ms. Bowman with an idea to create a family tree depicting the names of each family member on her mother's side, the countries from which they came, and the date of their arrival. Candice believes this would demonstrate her knowledge of the score 3.0 content.

4. Mr. McKimm is teaching a unit on quadratic equations. He writes an equation and its solution on the blackboard and asks the class to vote on whether the solution is correct or incorrect. He chooses one student to explain why he or she thinks the solution is correct and one to explain why he or she thinks the solution is incorrect. After hearing both sides, the students vote again. Mr. McKimm makes a mental note of how many students appear to understand the problem.

5. Ms. Walker is teaching a unit on volleyball. After covering individual skills with the students, she has split them up into teams. During one of the games, she notices that Ashley executes a perfect overhand serve. Ashley has had trouble with this skill, receiving low scores in the past. After seeing the serve, Ms. Walker makes a mental note to assign Ashley a higher score in the gradebook.

Exercise 2.3

Review Questions

The following questions deal with much of the important content in this chapter. Answer each one and then compare your answers with those provided on the corresponding answer sheet.

1. What are the three types of classroom assessment, and what are some of the unique qualities of each?

2. What are the three ways to use assessments, and what are some of the unique characteristics of each?

3. What is the difference between formative assessment and formative scores as defined in *Formative Assessment and Standards-Based Grading*?

4. Describe how assessments can provide information to teachers about their own performances.

Chapter 3

THE NEED FOR A NEW SCALE

As described in chapter 2, a defining characteristic of the process of formative assessment is that it uses formative scores to track student progress over time, leading to an estimate of a summative score. It makes intuitive sense that formative scores for a given topic would gradually increase over time—as students learn more about a topic, their scores go up. To illustrate, assume that formative scores are being collected for the topic of balancing equations in a middle school classroom. In the beginning, those formative scores would probably be relatively low, since many or most students have not had much experience solving algebraic equations of the form: $4 \cdot x = 48$. However, as time progresses, scores would likely improve. For example, on the first assessment, a student receives a score of 50. On the next assessment, the student receives a score of 60, and so on, until the final assessment of the unit produces a formative score of 74.

From this example, designing assessments that produce formative scores appears to be fairly straightforward. All a teacher has to do is design assessments, score them, and then keep track of students' scores during the time instruction is occurring. Unfortunately, there are some easy traps to fall into that can render the formative scores collected meaningless. One of the biggest traps is the improper use of the 100-point scale.

The 100-Point Scale

It is probably safe to assume that many, if not most, teachers use the 100-point scale as the basis for their assessments. This is primarily because it is fairly easy to translate any assessment into such a scale. To illustrate, assume that a teacher creates an assessment that has twelve multiple-choice items. If a student gets nine out of twelve items correct, the student receives a score of 75. To obtain this score, the teacher simply translates the ratio of the number of correct items divided by the total number of items into a decimal and then multiplies by one hundred ($9/12 = 0.75 \times 100 = 75$). Similarly, on the next assessment, the teacher might design five word problems, each of which are assigned points. The first two problems might be worth 10 points and the next three problems might be worth 15 points each, for a total of 65 points. Students' answers would be assigned points on each of the problems. To compute a score, the teacher simply adds up the number of points obtained by a student, divides by the total number of points available, and multiplies by one hundred. For example, assume a particular student received the following points for the five word problems: 7, 7, 11, 10, and 15. The student's score would be 77 ($50/65 = 0.77 \times 100 = 77$).

Thus far, there would seem to be no problem with this approach. However, close scrutiny of the 100-point scale discloses some significant issues. To illustrate, assume that you have designed an assessment with three parts—section A, section B, and section C. Section A contains ten multiple-choice items (items 1–10) that are factual in nature but very important to the topic being addressed. Section B contains four items (items 11–14) that address more complex content like generalizations and principles. These four items ask students to explain a principle or give examples of a generalization that was addressed in class. As such, they are not multiple-choice items. Instead, they require students to write a short constructed response. Section C contains two items only (items 15–16). These items require students to go one step further and make inferences and applications that go above and beyond what was addressed in class.

To demonstrate the potential problem posed by the 100-point scale, take a moment and assign points to the three sections of this assessment. In the spaces provided, record the points you assigned. Do not read any further until you have assigned points to each section, making sure that the points for sections A, B, and C sum up to 100. Table 3.1 provides a brief reminder of the characteristics of the items in the three sections.

Table 3.1 Types of Content in Three Sections of an Assessment

Section A:	Ten multiple-choice items that are factual in nature but important to the topic
Section B:	Four short constructed-response items that require students to explain principles or give examples of generalizations as presented in class
Section C:	Two short constructed-response items that require students to make inferences and applications that go beyond what was presented in class

Points for section A: _____

Points for section B: _____

Points for section C: _____

Total: _100_

Now that you have assigned points to each section, assume that a particular student has exhibited the following pattern of scores: he or she answered all of the items in section A correctly, two of the four items in section B correctly, and neither of the two items correctly in section C. Using the points you assigned to the three sections, compute the student's overall score. To do this, simply add up all the points you assigned to section A, half the points you assigned to section B, and none of the points you assigned to section C. To illustrate, if you assigned 40 points to section A, 40 points to section B, and 20 points to section C, the student's total points would be 60. Take a moment to compute the student's overall score using your scheme, and record it in the space provided.

Student's overall score: _____

Thousands of teachers have completed this activity in the context of workshops on classroom assessment. Table 3.2 depicts some common response patterns we have observed when administering this exercise.

Table 3.2 Common Response Patterns

	Points Assigned Section A	Points Assigned Section B	Points Assigned Section C	Total Points for Student (Final Score)
Teacher 1	40	40	20	60
Teacher 2	20	40	40	40
Teacher 3	60	20	20	70
Teacher 4	70	20	10	80
Teacher 5	20	20	60	30

As table 3.2 illustrates, the differences in the total points or final scores are dramatic. The range of total points for a student who answered all the items correctly on section A, half the items correctly in section B, and none of the items correctly in section C is 50 points (the low score in the right-hand column of table 3.2 is 30, and the high score is 80). Across the thousands of teachers who have completed this weighting exercise, the lowest score we have observed is 15, and the highest score is 90—a range of 75 points. To sum up, even though all the teachers were looking at the same pattern of responses for the items in the test, the differences in how they weighted each section of the assessment created a 75-point range.

The wide range of scores depicted in table 3.2 is not a simple artifact of this particular exercise. Studies have demonstrated that when teachers design their own assessments and assign points to the items in those assessments, students can obtain very different total scores from teacher to teacher simply because the teachers weight items differently (see Marzano, 2002). For example, Haponstall (2009) described a study in which 557 teachers all graded one paper using the 100-point scale. While the majority of the scores were between 59 and 73, scores ranged from 38 to 91 (pp. 27–28). Guskey and Bailey (2001) commented on a similar study conducted in 1912 in which copies of two English exam papers were graded by 142 teachers. As noted by Guskey and Bailey: "For one paper, the scores varied from 64 to 98. The other paper received scores ranging from 50 to 97. One of the papers was given a failing mark (a score of 75 is passing) by 15% of teachers, while 12% gave the same paper a grade of more than 90 points" (p. 26). Later, the same researchers repeated the study with mathematics and found even more variation.

This range in scores is a tremendous source of error associated with the 100-point scale. The inconsistent patterns of item weighting do not just exist between teachers, though; they exist between assessments designed by a single teacher as well. For example, on one test, a teacher might use items that are all very easy, and many of the students receive high scores. On the next test, most of the items might be very difficult, and many of the students receive low scores. Because there is no reflection of the level of difficulty of each assessment or between assessments, tracking student progress over time using formative scores becomes difficult if not impossible. In effect, weighting items differently from assessment to assessment and being uneven in the level of difficulty of items constituting each assessment is akin to changing the scale that is used from one assessment to the next. To use a simile, it is like measuring the physical growth of a student throughout the year but using a measuring tape that changes how long an inch is from one measurement to the next.

Clearly, a better method for developing and scoring assessments is needed—one that ensures that the scale (the size of an inch) stays the same from one assessment to the next and that a teacher applies the same logic to scoring each assessment. As the preceding discussion illustrates, such a method would exclude the typical use of the 100-point scale.

A Rigorous Rubric-Based Approach

The concept of a rubric has been around for many years. Although the term is used in a variety of ways in the assessment community, its roots can be traced to the Latin *rubica terra*, referring to the use of red earth centuries ago to mark or signify something of importance. In the assessment world today, the term *rubric* usually applies to a description of knowledge or skill for a specific topic like that shown in table 3.3.

Table 3.3 A Rubric for the Social Studies Topic of World War II at Grade 6

4	The student will create and defend a hypothesis about what might have happened if specific events that led to World War II had not happened or had happened differently.
3	The student will compare the primary causes for World War II with the primary causes for World War I.
2	The student will describe the primary causes for World War II.
1	The student will recognize isolated facts about World War II.

To a great extent, rubrics resemble learning progressions as described by Heritage (2008). Recall from the discussion in chapter 1 that learning progressions describe content relative to a specific topic in increasingly more sophisticated levels of knowledge or skill. The rubric in table 3.3 describes increasingly more complex knowledge regarding World War II.

While rubrics like that in table 3.3 have been used successfully in classrooms for years, if they are not utilized to their full capacity, they can have some of the same disadvantages as the 100-point scale when it comes to providing formative scores for students. To illustrate, consider table 3.4, which is a rubric written by a different teacher on the same topic and for the same grade level as the rubric in table 3.3.

Table 3.4 A Second Rubric Regarding World War II at Grade 6

4	The student will compare the turning points in World War II to those in other wars.
3	The student will discuss key turning points in World War II that led to the victory of the Allied powers.
2	The student will recall basic information about how the Allied powers achieved a victory in World War II.
1	The student will recognize basic information about the outcome of World War II.

Notice that even though the rubrics address the same topic (World War II), they have very different expectations regarding the content for scores 2, 3, and 4. In the first rubric (table 3.3), the score 3 content asks students to compare the causes of World War II with those of World War I. The score 3 content in the second rubric (table 3.4) asks students to discuss the turning points in World War II. This content is somewhat easier than the score 3 content in the first rubric.

In general, the content in the first rubric is more complex at each level than the content in the second rubric. Discrepancies like this occur when schools simply tell teachers to design rubrics without providing guidance regarding how to do so. In such a system, teacher rubrics will be very different from teacher to teacher.

To solve the problem of inconsistent rubrics from teacher to teacher, it is necessary to develop a systematic approach to rubric design. In the books *Classroom Assessment and Grading That Work* (Marzano, 2006) and *Making Standards Useful in the Classroom* (Marzano & Haystead, 2008), a case is made that teams of teachers and/or curriculum specialists representing the district or school should design the rubrics for the content at each grade level and provide them to teachers. This is certainly the best approach to rubric design and is recommended highly. Simply put, the most powerful approach is for a district or school to provide teachers with the rubrics to be used over an entire year for a given subject area.

If a district or school does not provide such resources for teachers, then individual teachers can and should design their own rubrics using a systematic approach. Just how to approach the design of rigorous rubrics is addressed in depth in the book *Designing and Teaching Learning Goals and Objectives* (Marzano, 2009). Here the topic is addressed briefly.

Identifying Simpler and More Complex Content

The first step in designing rigorous rubrics is to identify one or more specific learning goals that will be the target of instruction. This can be done for each unit. Ideally, a teacher would construct learning goals for an entire year. To illustrate, assume that a science teacher is preparing for a unit on heredity. He or she might identify the following two learning goals:

> Learning goal 1: Students will be able to differentiate heritable traits from nonheritable traits in real-world scenarios.
>
> Learning goal 2: Students will be able to make predictions using the Mendelian square.

The next thing the teacher would do is to identify some simpler content and more complex content for each of those learning goals. This is shown for the first learning goal:

> More complex content for learning goal 1: Students will be able to discuss how heritable traits and nonheritable traits affect one another.
>
> Learning goal 1: Students will be able to differentiate heritable traits from nonheritable traits in real-world scenarios.
>
> Simpler content for learning goal 1: Students will be able to recognize accurate statements about and isolated examples of heritable and nonheritable traits.

Notice that for the first learning goal, the simpler content requires students to simply recognize facts about heritable traits and nonheritable traits. It does not require differentiating between these two types of traits as does the target learning goal. The content is obviously easier than that specified by the learning goal. Conversely, the more complex content requires students to go beyond the expectation of the target goal by requiring students to discuss how heritable traits and nonheritable traits affect one another.

The content related to the second learning goal would follow the same pattern:

> More complex content for learning goal 2: Students will be able to discuss the role of genetics in diseases such as diabetes.

Learning goal 2: Students will be able to make predictions using the Mendelian square.

Simpler content for learning goal 2: Students will recall facts about the Mendelian square.

Exercise 3.1 provides some practice in identifying simpler and more complex content for learning goals. (See page 55 for a reproducible of this exercise and page 137 for a reproducible answer sheet. Visit **marzanoresearch.com/classroomstrategiesthatwork** to download all the exercises and answers in this book.)

Exercise 3.1
Simpler and More Complex Content for Learning Goals

For each of the following learning goals from five different subject areas, use the spaces provided to write content that is more complex and content that is simpler, and then compare your answers with those provided on the corresponding answer sheet.

Learning goal 1: Students will be able to multiply two-digit numbers by two-digit numbers.

More complex content: _____

Simpler content: _____

Learning goal 2: Students will be able to label the world's continents on a map.

More complex content: _____

Simpler content: _____

Learning goal 3: Students will be able to sing with correct tempo and pitch.

More complex content: _____

Simpler content: _____

Learning goal 4: Students will be able to discuss the major cause-and-effect relationships in a narrative story.

More complex content: _____

Simpler content: _____

Learning goal 5: Students will be able to discuss how the earth changes through both fast processes and slow processes.

More complex content: _____

Simpler content: _____

Designing a Scale

With a learning goal and its associated simpler and more complex content established, a teacher can design a rigorous rubric or scale. Because it is technically more accurate to use the word *scale* than the term *rubric*, in the remainder of the text we use the word *scale*. As described in *Classroom Assessment and Grading That Work* (Marzano, 2006), a scale is an attempt to create a continuum that articulates distinct levels of knowledge and skill relative to a specific topic. Again, a well-written scale can be thought of as an applied version of a learning progression. Additionally, a well-written scale should make it easy for teachers to design and score assessments that can be used to generate both formative scores and summative scores.

The generic form of the scale recommended in this book is depicted in table 3.5 (page 45).

Table 3.5 Generic Form of the Scale

Score 4.0	More complex content
Score 3.0	Target learning goal
Score 2.0	Simpler content
Score 1.0	With help, partial success at score 2.0 content and score 3.0 content
Score 0.0	Even with help, no success

To understand the scale, it is best to start with score 3.0. To receive a score of 3.0, a student must demonstrate competence regarding the target learning goal. A score of 2.0 indicates competence regarding the simpler content, and a score of 4.0 indicates competence regarding the more complex content. Scores 4.0, 3.0, and 2.0 involve different content, then, while scores 1.0 and 0.0 do not. A score of 1.0 indicates that, independently, a student cannot demonstrate competence in the score 2.0 or 3.0 content, but, with help, he or she demonstrates partial competence. Score 0.0 indicates that even with help, a student does not demonstrate competence or skill in any of the content.

Table 3.6 uses one of the learning goals about heritable traits described previously to show what a scale that has been filled in might look like.

Table 3.6 Scale for Goal 1

Score 4.0	Students will be able to discuss how heritable traits and nonheritable traits affect one another.
Score 3.0	Students will be able to differentiate heritable traits from nonheritable traits in real-world scenarios.
Score 2.0	Students will be able to recognize accurate statements about and isolated examples of heritable and nonheritable traits.
Score 1.0	With help, partial success at score 2.0 content and score 3.0 content
Score 0.0	Even with help, no success

Again, the score 3.0 content is the target learning goal. Thus, a teacher simply uses the target learning goal for the class as the score 3.0 content when designing a scale. The next whole-point score down is 2.0. The simpler content goes here. The next whole-point score up from the target learning goal (score 3.0) is 4.0. The more complex content goes there.

The score values of 1.0 and 0.0 do not represent new content, but they do represent different levels of competence. Score 1.0 indicates that the student does not demonstrate competence in any of the content when working independently. However, with help, the student has partial success at the score 2.0 and score 3.0 content. Score 0.0 indicates that even with help, the student has no success at the score 3.0 or 2.0 content.

Writing Scales in Student-Friendly Language

The scales described in the preceding text are written for the teacher; they are in teacher-friendly language. To make scales more useful to students, they should be written in student-friendly language. This should be done in cooperation with students. The teacher should introduce each scale to students as it is used in class; explain what is meant by the content placed at the score values 4.0, 3.0, and 2.0;

and then have the entire class participate in rewriting the content at each score value in a manner that makes it easy for students to understand. To illustrate, consider again the scale in table 3.6 (page 45). The teacher would start with the score 3.0 content, explaining his or her expectations for it. Once students had a firm grasp of the score 3.0 content (the target learning goal), he or she would explain expectations for the score 2.0 and 4.0 content. Next, students would be asked to work in small groups to come up with their own ways of wording the score 2.0, 3.0, and 4.0 content. These suggestions would be put together into a rewritten version of the scale that might resemble table 3.7.

Table 3.7 Student-Friendly Scale

Score 4.0	We should be able to talk about how the traits we inherit and the traits we develop on our own are related to one another. For example, a person born in a family that has always lived near the equator might have darker skin and enjoy warm-weather hobbies such as swimming or scuba diving, but someone born in a family that has always lived in a cold climate might have fair skin and enjoy cold-weather hobbies such as skiing or ice skating.
Score 3.0	We should be able to tell the difference between traits we inherit from our parents and traits we develop on our own. For example, Michael Phelps is such a good swimmer partly because of how tall he is and how wide his wingspan is (traits he inherited) and partly because he practiced really hard and did what his coach told him to (things he chose to do).
Score 2.0	We should be able to talk about the traits we get from our parents and the traits we develop on our own. For example, we cannot change the traits we get from our parents, such as height or eye color, but we can change the traits we develop, such as patience or work ethic.
Score 1.0	With help, partial success at score 2.0 content and score 3.0 content
Score 0.0	Even with help, no success

Notice that the rewritten scale has examples of what it would look like to provide a correct answer for the score 2.0, 3.0, and 4.0 content. This is critical to student-friendly scales. In effect, the teacher and the students have created something akin to what composition teachers refer to as an "anchor paper." In the context of writing instruction, an anchor paper is a composition that clearly shows the characteristics that are expected of a particular type of composition. The same is true of the examples for the score 2.0, 3.0, and 4.0 content in table 3.7. The student-friendly scales should provide students with clear guidance as to what it would look like to demonstrate score 2.0, 3.0, and 4.0 competence.

Using the Scales to Score Assessments

With scales written for the unit-specific learning goals, a teacher can design and score various types of assessments. We go into this process in depth in chapter 4. Briefly though, consider again the scale shown in table 3.7. To assess the content in this scale, a teacher might design a test like the one in table 3.8.

Notice that the test is organized into three sections—one for score 2.0 content (section A), one for score 3.0 content (section B), and one for score 4.0 content (section C). To score this assessment, the teacher would look at the pattern of responses across the three sections. If a student correctly answered all items on the test, she would receive a score of 4.0. If she answered all items correctly in sections A and B but not section C, she would receive a score of 3.0. If she answered all of the items correctly in section A but not B and C, she would receive a score of 2.0. If she could answer no items correctly on her own but could answer some items correctly with help from the teacher, she would receive a score of 1.0. Finally, the score of 0.0 would be assigned if she could answer no items correctly, even with help.

Table 3.8 Sample Test

Section A
1. True or False: All diseases are inherited. _____
2. True or False: If your mom is afraid of roller coasters, you will inherit that fear from her. _____
3. Examples of inherited traits are _____ and _____.
4. Put a check in front of the traits you can develop over time.
_____ Shoe size
_____ Gender
_____ Knowledge of history
_____ Fear of snakes

Section B
5. Name three traits you like about yourself. Are these heritable traits or not? Explain your answer.
_____
_____
6. Joey signed up for the summer spelling bee just after Christmas. He did not practice very much because he was playing baseball, and he went to Florida with his parents over spring break. When the bee came, he lost in the first round. Later that night, he told his mother he lost because he is not very smart about words. Do you think this is correct? Why or why not?
_____
_____
7. Simon's mother always asks him to go to the grocery store with her so that he can reach the items on the top shelf. He can reach almost everything she points out. Is this because Simon was born tall, or is it because he has so much practice reaching for items in high places? Has he inherited his ability to reach items on the top shelf? Explain your answer.
_____
_____

Section C
8. Hemophilia is an inherited disease that prevents your blood from clotting. This means that if you ever get a cut or a scrape, you might lose so much blood that it could be life threatening. If you were born with this disease, what kinds of things would you have to avoid? What kinds of things might you be good at instead? What kinds of personality traits might you have that other people might not have? Explain your answer.
_____
_____

You probably see a problem with scoring this test right away. What if the student answers all score 2.0 questions (section A) and some of the score 3.0 questions (section B) correctly? Does the student receive a score of 2.0 or 3.0? The solution to this dilemma lies in the use of a scale that employs half-point scores. This is depicted in table 3.9 (page 48).

Now the scale is sensitive to partial credit or to some items answered incorrectly for a particular section of an assessment. Again, it is useful to begin with the target goal—score 3.0 content. A score of 3.0 indicates that a student has answered all 3.0 items correctly. A score of 2.5 means that the student has success at the score 2.0 content (the simpler content) and has partial success at the score 3.0 content (the target learning goal). A score of 3.5 indicates that a student has success at the 3.0 content (the target learning goal) and partial success at the 4.0 content (the more complex content). A score of 1.5

indicates that a student has partial success at the score 2.0 content (the simpler learning goal). Finally, a score of 0.5 indicates that, with help, a student has partial success at the score 2.0 content.

Table 3.9 Complete Scale

Score 4.0	More complex content
Score 3.5	In addition to score 3.0 performance, partial success at score 4.0 content
Score 3.0	Target learning goal
Score 2.5	No major errors or omissions regarding score 2.0 content, and partial success at score 3.0 content
Score 2.0	Simpler content
Score 1.5	Partial success at score 2.0 content, but major errors or omissions regarding score 3.0 content
Score 1.0	With help, partial success at score 2.0 content and score 3.0 content
Score 0.5	With help, partial success at score 2.0 content, but not at score 3.0 content
Score 0.0	Even with help, no success

Over the years, we have found that teachers can use this scale to design and score classroom assessments with a relatively high degree of reliability (see Marzano, 2002). To illustrate, let us go back to the activity you completed regarding the inadequacies of the 100-point scale. Table 3.10 reproduces the content of the three sections of the hypothetical assessment.

Table 3.10 Types of Content in Three Sections of an Assessment

Section A:	Ten multiple-choice items that are factual in nature but important to the topic
Section B:	Four short constructed-response items that require students to explain principles or give examples of generalizations as presented in class
Section C:	Two short constructed-response items that require students to make inferences and applications that go beyond what was presented in class

Recall that you were asked to compute a score for a student who answered all items correctly in section A, half of the items correctly in section B, and no items correctly in section C. As described previously, when the 100-point scale is used to score this pattern of responses, scores will range from 15 to 90 due to the differential weighting of items. Teachers assign scores with much less variability when the scale in table 3.9 is used, especially when they realize that section A items represent score 2.0 content, section B items represent score 3.0 content, and section C items represent score 4.0 content. In fact, scoring is quite straightforward from this new perspective. The student has answered all score 2.0 items correctly and half of score 3.0 items correctly. Therefore, the student receives a score of 2.5.

The preceding example involves a traditional paper/pencil test, but the scale applies equally well with other types of assessments. For example, an art teacher might design an assessment for which students are asked to sketch an object of their choice. However, in the directions, students are asked to make sure they demonstrate a sense of the basic sketching technique addressed in class (score 2.0 content), demonstrate an awareness of the concept of perspective as addressed in class (score 3.0 content), and demonstrate orally or through writing how they have modified some of the basic techniques to achieve a specific artistic purpose (score 4.0 content).

To score a sketch, the teacher would first make sure that the student had demonstrated the basic sketching techniques. If so, the teacher would know that his score was at least 2.0. The teacher would next examine his approach to perspective (score 3.0 content). If he had partial success with using the principles of perspective, a score of 2.5 would be assigned. If his sketch exemplified the principles of perspective with no major errors or omissions, a score of 3.0 would be assigned, and so on.

Exercise 3.2 provides some practice in scoring assessments using the scale. (See page 56 for a reproducible of this exercise and page 139 for a reproducible answer sheet. Visit **marzanoresearch.com/classroomstrategiesthatwork** to download all the exercises and answers in this book.)

Exercise 3.2 Scoring Assessments Using the Scale

Following are different patterns of response for different types of assessments. Score these assessments using the scale depicted in table 3.9 (page 48).

1. Mr. Swanson has set up an activity that allows the students in his physical education class to demonstrate their ability to balance themselves. Some parts of the activity ask students to demonstrate the simpler aspects of the goal (score 2.0 content), such as approaching the balancing activity slowly and with a firm foundation. Other parts of the activity ask students to demonstrate target behaviors, such as walking on a balance beam (score 3.0 content), and some parts of the activity ask students to demonstrate behaviors above and beyond the target learning goal, such as throwing a ball to a partner while balancing or catching themselves when they begin to fall (score 4.0 content). Bonnie exhibits ability in the simpler balance activities and has some success at the target balance activities. Her score is _____. Explain your answer.

2. For a learning goal regarding speaking fluency, Mrs. Jass has assigned the students in her French class a brief oral report on the topic of food. Students must use some basic vocabulary words relevant to the topic (score 2.0 content). They must also use complete sentences to discuss how French meal habits are different from the meal habits in the United States (score 3.0 content). Finally, Mrs. Jass asks them to offer a few sentences about which food culture (French or American) they prefer and why (score 4.0 content). Ida exhibits the ability to pronounce the relevant vocabulary words provided and the ability to speak in simple sentences about the topic clearly and fluently. Though she does not have a strong opinion on the topic, she clearly expresses the advantages of each culture. Her score is _____. Explain your answer.

3. Mr. Gage has assigned a short language arts paper that will allow him to assess his students on a learning goal regarding the use of research in a persuasive composition. In the directions, he has provided a topic and asked the students to take one of two possible positions. In order to persuade the audience, he has asked them to find two valid research sources (score 2.0 content). He has also asked them to use direct quotations from those sources to support their chosen positions (score 3.0 content). Finally, he has asked that they address any possible counterclaims they see as relevant (score 4.0 content). Caroline's assignment demonstrates that she has found two valid sources of support for her chosen position; however, while the composition mentions both of those sources, it does not directly quote either, and no counterclaim is addressed. Her score is _____. Explain your answer.

4. Ms. Satrom has noticed that Jasper did not do well on a particular mathematics test. The test asked the students to read a word problem and translate it into a mathematical equation (score 2.0 content), solve the equation (score 3.0 content), and compare the final answer to the original word problem to see if the answer makes sense (score 4.0 content). She calls Jasper in for an individual meeting and goes through one of the problems with him. While he was not able to solve the problem on his own, he is able to create a mathematical equation and solve it with some guidance and prompting from Ms. Satrom. His score is _____. Explain your answer.

5. Mr. Kitchens has created a role-play activity to assess his social studies students' knowledge about American presidents. He has provided directions for the role play, giving students three presidents from whom to choose. After choosing one president, the students must create a scene that delivers personal facts about the president and the time in which he was in office (score 2.0 content). Students must also depict the president making one of his most influential choices (score 3.0 content). Finally, the scene must depict the president considering making a choice different from the one he made (score 4.0 content). Sally delivers the relevant information about the president she chose but depicts his character making a choice only the current president has encountered—not a choice her selected president had to make. She does not depict any other choices that the selected president could have made. Her score is _____. Explain your answer.

Over the years of using this scale, we have found that some teachers prefer to make an even finer distinction than half-point scores. Specifically, the half-point scale does not make a fine enough distinction of partial credit for some teachers. For example, assume a teacher has designed an assessment with ten items that address score 2.0 content. Also assume that one student has answered seven of these items correctly and another student has answered three of the items correctly. Neither student has answered score 3.0 or 4.0 items correctly. Using the scale with the half-point scores, both students would probably receive a score of 1.5, but this score does not reflect the fact that one student answered 70 percent of the score 2.0 items correctly and the other student answered 30 percent of the score 2.0 items correctly. The scale in table 3.11 addresses the issue.

Table 3.11 One-Third Interval Scores

Score 4.0	More complex learning goal
Score 3.67	In addition to score 3.0 performance, high partial success at score 4.0 content
Score 3.33	In addition to score 3.0 performance, low partial success at score 4.0 content
Score 3.0	Target learning goal
Score 2.67	No major errors or omissions regarding score 2.0 content, and high partial success at score 3.0 content
Score 2.33	No major errors or omissions regarding score 2.0 content, and low partial success at score 3.0 content
Score 2.0	Simpler learning goal
Score 1.67	High partial success at score 2.0 content, but major errors or omissions regarding score 3.0 content
Score 1.33	Low partial success at score 2.0 content, but major errors or omissions regarding score 3.0 content
Score 1.0	With help, partial success at score 2.0 content and score 3.0 content
Score 0.5	With help, partial success at score 2.0 content, but not at score 3.0 content
Score 0.0	Even with help, no success

In table 3.11, one-third intervals are used between whole-point scores. This allows for finer discrimination of partial credit. A score of 3.67 means that a student has demonstrated complete success with the score 3.0 content and high partial success with the 4.0 content. A score of 3.33 means that a student has demonstrated complete success with score 3.0 content and low partial success with score 4.0 content. Likewise, a score of 2.67 means that a student has demonstrated complete success with score 2.0 content and high partial success with score 3.0 content. A score of 2.33 means that a student has demonstrated complete success with score 2.0 content and low partial success with the score 3.0 content.

This solves the problem of scoring the assessments that belong to the two students who answered three items and seven items correctly for the score 2.0 content. The student who answered three items correctly would receive a score of 1.33, indicating low partial success with the score 2.0 content, and the student who answered seven items correctly would receive a score of 1.67, indicating high partial success. Occasionally, some teachers have modified the scale even further. Instead of one-third intervals, they use one-quarter intervals. That is, a score of 1.25 indicates low partial success at the score 2.0 content, a score of 1.50 indicates partial success that is right in the middle of the interval, and a score of 1.75 indicates high partial success.

It is important to note in table 3.11 that the 0.0–1.0 interval uses a half-point score (0.5) as opposed to scores of 0.33 and 0.67. This is because teachers have reported that it is very difficult to make distinctions any finer than a half-point interval when providing help to students.

One further comment should be made about the scale presented in this chapter. Over the years of seeing it used, we have observed many adaptations and variations, some of which are described in *Classroom Assessment and Grading That Work* (Marzano, 2006) and *Making Standards Useful in the Classroom* (Marzano & Haystead, 2008). For example, some uses of the scale do not identify score 4.0 content. Rather, the expectation for score 4.0 is that students make adaptations and inferences that go beyond what was explicitly taught at the score 3.0 level. This lack of specificity at score 4.0 provides many options for students to demonstrate competency beyond the score 3.0 level.

Using Preexisting Assessments

In the next chapter (chapter 4), we consider how classroom assessments can be designed in such a way as to mirror the scale described in this chapter. However, many teachers find themselves in a situation where they want to use or have to use assessments that were not designed with the scale in mind. This should not be considered a problem. A teacher simply has to interpret these other assessments in terms of the scale. Here, we consider three different situations in which a translation might be used.

Using a Preexisting Test

A teacher might have access to traditional tests that he or she would like to continue to use. Traditional obtrusive assessments that use a paper/pencil format are fairly easy to translate into the 0–4-point scale. To illustrate, consider the assessment in table 3.12, which might have been an assessment designed by a school or district as a common assessment for a lower-elementary science class on the topic of properties of earth materials.

Table 3.12 Common Assessment for Properties of Earth Materials

1. Three earth materials that humans use are _____, _____, and _____.
2. How do humans use each of those materials?
3. Three characteristics of soil are _____, _____, and _____.
4. Using the three characteristics listed above, briefly describe one of the soils we studied in class this week. Where can you find that soil, and why do you think it has those particular characteristics?

5. Most fossils are:
  A. Decades old
  B. Hundreds of years old
  C. Millions of years old
  D. None of the above

6. Briefly describe two things we can learn from fossils. _____

The assessment in table 3.12 has six items that were designed to be scored on the basis of points. To translate this into an assessment that can be scored using the scale, a teacher need only classify the six items into three categories representing score 2.0 content, score 3.0 content, and score 4.0 content, respectively. The teacher might decide that items 1, 3, and 5 qualify as score 2.0 content because they represent basic factual knowledge. Items 2, 4, and 6 might be classified as score 3.0 content, as they address more complex content. In some cases, a preexisting assessment must be augmented to meet the requirements of the scale introduced in this chapter. For example, the preexisting assessment in table 3.12 has a number of items that represent 2.0 and 3.0 content but no items that represent score 4.0 content (no items in the assessment ask the student to make inferences beyond what was taught in class). The teacher would simply add some score 4.0 items to the test and then score the assessment in the manner described previously by examining the pattern of response across the items.

Using a Preexisting Rubric

Many schools and districts have developed rubrics to be used in specific situations. For example, some states and districts employ a variation of the six-trait writing rubrics designed by the Northwest Regional Educational Laboratory (www.thetraits.org/index.php). That system employs a rubric with six levels for each of six traits: voice, ideas and content, sentence fluency, word choice, organization, and conventions. To illustrate the basic structure of the 6-point scale, consider table 3.13, which is modeled after the rubric for the trait of organization.

Table 3.13 Scale for the Trait of Organization

Level	Characteristics	Translation to Score on Scale
Not Yet	The writing lacks a sense of coherence, as exhibited by a lack of effective sequences or a lack of organization.	1.0 or below
Emerging	The writing lacks a clear organizational structure, but some rudimentary organizational devices are in place.	1.5
		2.0
Developing	A skeletal organizational structure is in place.	2.5
Competent	Organizational structure is clear but formulaic.	3.0
Experienced	Organizational structure is clear, is not formulaic, and enhances the main idea.	3.5
Wow	Organizational structure is compelling and clearly enhances the coherence of the writing.	4.0

To adapt this rubric to the 0–4-point scale presented in this chapter, a teacher must only equate levels of the existing rubric with specific score values on the scale. In table 3.13, the teacher has equated the level of Not Yet with a score of 1.0 or below (see the last column, titled Translation to Score on Scale). The score of 1.0 means that, with help, the student can perform some of the target procedures. In this case, if a student received a score of Not Yet on the rubric, the teacher would have to make a judgment about what (if anything) the student could do with help. This would no doubt require some interaction with the student.

The score of Emerging on the rubric has been equated to the scale score of 1.5 or 2.0. Again, for an individual student's composition, a teacher would have to make a determination if the score of Emerging represented a complete demonstration of the simpler aspects of organization (score 2.0) or a partial demonstration of the simpler aspects of organization (score 1.5). In table 3.13, the levels of Developing, Competent, Experienced, and Wow have all been equated to single values of the scale scores, which should make for a fairly easy translation.

As this example illustrates, a teacher simply determines which levels of the preexisting rubric equate to specific scale scores when converting a preexisting rubric to scale scores. In some cases, a score on a preexisting rubric might be interpreted as more than one score value on the scale. In table 3.13, this is the case with the scores of Not Yet and Emerging. The teacher must keep this in mind when scoring students using the preexisting rubric. In such cases, teachers typically develop a personal coding scheme to indicate if Not Yet (for example) means that a student can produce no organizational structure even with help (the student should receive a scale score of 0.0), a student can produce some of the simpler aspects of an organizational structure with help (the student should receive a scale score of 0.5), or a student can produce some of the simpler aspects and some of the more sophisticated aspects of an organizational structure with help (the student should receive a scale score of 1.0).

Using Preexisting Learning Progressions

Some teachers might work in a school or district that has developed learning progressions like the one by Herman and Choi (2008, p. 7) described in chapter 1 (page 11). The scale easily accommodates this situation also. To illustrate, let us consider the six-level progression for the topic of buoyancy presented in chapter 1. All six levels can be mapped into the 0–4-point scale as shown in table 3.14.

Table 3.14 Scale for a Preexisting Learning Progression

Score 4.0	Student knows that floating depends on having less density than the medium.
Score 3.5	Student knows that floating depends on having a small density.
Score 3.0	Student knows that floating depends on having a small mass and a large volume.
Score 2.5	Student knows that floating depends on having a small mass, or student knows that floating depends on having a large volume.
Score 2.0	Student thinks that floating depends on having a small size, heft, or amount, or that it depends on being made out of a particular material.
Score 1.5	Student thinks that floating depends on being flat, hollow, filled with air, or having holes.
Score 1.0	With help, partial success at score 2.0 content and score 3.0 content
Score 0.5	With help, partial success at score 2.0 content, but not at score 3.0 content
Score 0.0	Even with help, no success

As shown in table 3.14, the lowest level of the learning progression occupies the score value of 1.5, and the highest level of the learning progression occupies the score value of 4.0. Each whole-point and half-point score value above 1.0 has content from the learning progression. It is important not to assign content to score values 1.0, 0.5, or 0.0. All of these represent student responses with help from the teacher. If a learning progression has more levels than can be accommodated by the half-point scale, the teacher can use the scale with one-third intervals or even the scale with quarter intervals.

Exercise 3.3 (page 54) provides some review questions for this chapter. (See page 58 for a reproducible of this exercise and page 141 for a reproducible answer sheet. Visit **marzanoresearch.com/classroom strategiesthatwork** to download all the exercises and answers in this book.)

Exercise 3.3
Review Questions

The following questions address much of the important content in the chapter. Answer each one and then compare your answers with those provided on the corresponding answer sheet.

1. What are some of the flaws of the 100-point scale?

2. Describe the basic process for writing a scale.

3. Why is it important for students to rewrite scales in their own words?

4. Describe how teachers can make use of preexisting assessments.

Summary

This chapter began with an activity designed to illustrate the flaws in the 100-point scale. The remainder of the chapter focused on the design and use of a rigorous rubric-based approach in the interest of valid and reliable assessing. Ideally, target learning goals and their accompanying scales should be designed at the school or district level to ensure consistency. If this is not possible, teachers should identify learning goals for the content addressed in their own units of instruction. Next, simpler content and more complex content are identified for each learning goal. These goals are then used to design scales. Once scales are designed, the class can work together to rewrite them into language that is easily accessible to everyone. Assessments can be designed based on the scales and scored consistently according to students' patterns of response. Typically, scales with half-point intervals are used, but teachers may use one-third or even one-quarter interval scales if they so choose. Finally, preexisting assessments and preexisting rubrics can be adapted to fit the scale.

Exercise 3.1

Simpler and More Complex Content for Learning Goals

For each of the following learning goals from five different subject areas, use the spaces provided to write content that is more complex and content that is simpler, and then compare your answers with those provided on the corresponding answer sheet.

Learning goal 1: Students will be able to multiply two-digit numbers by two-digit numbers.

More complex content: _____

Simpler content: _____

Learning goal 2: Students will be able to label the world's continents on a map.

More complex content: _____

Simpler content: _____

Learning goal 3: Students will be able to sing with correct tempo and pitch.

More complex content: _____

Simpler content: _____

Learning goal 4: Students will be able to discuss the major cause-and-effect relationships in a narrative story.

More complex content: _____

Simpler content: _____

Learning goal 5: Students will be able to discuss how the earth changes through both fast processes and slow processes.

More complex content: _____

Simpler content: _____

Exercise 3.2

Scoring Assessments Using the Scale

Following are different patterns of response for different types of assessments. Score these assessments using the scale depicted in table 3.9 (page 48).

1. Mr. Swanson has set up an activity that allows the students in his physical education class to demonstrate their ability to balance themselves. Some parts of the activity ask students to demonstrate the simpler aspects of the goal (score 2.0 content), such as approaching the balancing activity slowly and with a firm foundation. Other parts of the activity ask students to demonstrate target behaviors, such as walking on a balance beam (score 3.0 content), and some parts of the activity ask students to demonstrate behaviors above and beyond the target learning goal, such as throwing a ball to a partner while balancing or catching themselves when they begin to fall (score 4.0 content). Bonnie exhibits ability in the simpler balance activities and has some success at the target balance activities. Her score is _____. Explain your answer.

2. For a learning goal regarding speaking fluency, Mrs. Jass has assigned the students in her French class a brief oral report on the topic of food. Students must use some basic vocabulary words relevant to the topic (score 2.0 content). They must also use complete sentences to discuss how French meal habits are different from the meal habits in the United States (score 3.0 content). Finally, Mrs. Jass asks them to offer a few sentences about which food culture (French or American) they prefer and why (score 4.0 content). Ida exhibits the ability to pronounce the relevant vocabulary words provided and the ability to speak in simple sentences about the topic clearly and fluently. Though she does not have a strong opinion on the topic, she clearly expresses the advantages of each culture. Her score is _____. Explain your answer.

3. Mr. Gage has assigned a short language arts paper that will allow him to assess his students on a learning goal regarding the use of research in a persuasive composition. In the directions, he has provided a topic and asked the students to take one of two possible positions. In order to persuade the audience, he has asked them to find two valid research sources (score 2.0 content). He has also asked them to use direct quotations from those sources to support their chosen positions (score 3.0 content). Finally, he has asked that they address any possible counterclaims they see as relevant (score 4.0 content). Caroline's assignment demonstrates that she has found two valid sources of support for her chosen position; however, while the composition mentions both of those sources, it does not directly quote either, and no counterclaim is addressed. Her score is _____. Explain your answer.

4. Ms. Satrom has noticed that Jasper did not do well on a particular mathematics test. The test asked the students to read a word problem and translate it into a mathematical equation (score 2.0 content), solve the equation (score 3.0 content),

Formative Assessment and Standards-Based Grading • © 2010 Marzano Research Laboratory • marzanoresearch.com
Visit **marzanoresearch.com/classroomstrategiesthatwork** to download this page.

and compare the final answer to the original word problem to see if the answer makes sense (score 4.0 content). She calls Jasper in for an individual meeting and goes through one of the problems with him. While he was not able to solve the problem on his own, he is able to create a mathematical equation and solve it with some guidance and prompting from Ms. Satrom. His score is _____. Explain your answer.

5. Mr. Kitchens has created a role-play activity to assess his social studies students' knowledge about American presidents. He has provided directions for the role play, giving students three presidents from whom to choose. After choosing one president, the students must create a scene that delivers personal facts about the president and the time in which he was in office (score 2.0 content). Students must also depict the president making one of his most influential choices (score 3.0 content). Finally, the scene must depict the president considering making a choice different from the one he made (score 4.0 content). Sally delivers the relevant information about the president she chose but depicts his character making a choice only the current president has encountered—not a choice her selected president had to make. She does not depict any other choices that the selected president could have made. Her score is _____. Explain your answer.

Formative Assessment and Standards-Based Grading • © 2010 Marzano Research Laboratory • marzanoresearch.com
Visit **marzanoresearch.com/classroomstrategiesthatwork** to download this page.

Exercise 3.3

Review Questions

The following questions address much of the important content in the chapter. Answer each one and then compare your answers with those provided on the corresponding answer sheet.

1. What are some of the flaws of the 100-point scale?

2. Describe the basic process for writing a scale.

3. Why is it important for students to rewrite scales in their own words?

4. Describe how teachers can make use of preexisting assessments.

Chapter 4

DESIGNING ASSESSMENTS

We saw in chapter 2 that assessments come in three formats: obtrusive assessments, unobtrusive assessments, and student-generated assessments. This chapter addresses how to design assessments across this spectrum. Because of their complexity and the frequency with which they are used, obtrusive assessments will be addressed first and in more depth. We begin with selected-response items in obtrusive assessments.

Selected-Response Items in Obtrusive Assessments

Selected-response items are commonly used in obtrusive assessments. They are referred to as selected response because they require students to select an answer from among a set of options. Common types of selected-response items are multiple choice, matching, alternative choice, true/false, multiple response, and fill in the blank. We consider each very briefly. For a more detailed discussion of these formats, see Marzano (2006).

Multiple Choice

Multiple-choice items provide a series of answers (typically four answers) from which students are to select the correct one. Table 4.1 (page 60) contains sample multiple-choice items for mathematics, language arts, science, and social studies.

Matching

Matching items require students to match elements of information that are related. Typically, more possible answers are offered than elements to which they are to be matched. Table 4.2 (pages 60–61) contains sample matching items for mathematics, language arts, science, and social studies.

Alternative Choice

Alternative-choice items are like multiple-choice items. However, they offer only two possible answers. Table 4.3 (page 61) contains sample alternative-choice items for mathematics, language arts, science, and social studies.

Table 4.1 Sample Multiple-Choice Items for Mathematics, Language Arts, Science, and Social Studies

Subject	Multiple-Choice Item
Mathematics	Which of the following fractions is equivalent to ¾? A. $^{75}/_{100}$ B. $^{18}/_{64}$ C. $^{8}/_{64}$ D. 3.4
Language arts	Which of the following sentences is punctuated correctly? A. He went to the store, because he needed milk. B. The sun was bright and Mike didn't have any sunglasses. C. Because the power had gone out, no one was able to watch television. D. Initially, Roger wanted to join the army, instead of going to college.
Science	Which of the following is an accurate statement about Venus? A. It is composed mostly of carbon dioxide. B. It is covered by thick clouds of sulfuric acid. C. It is believed to have had water that has all boiled away. D. It is surrounded by rings.
Social studies	The best definition of immigration is: A. Entering a new country to settle permanently B. Moving from one neighborhood to another C. Driving through one state to get to another D. Traveling from one country to another on vacation

Table 4.2 Sample Matching Items for Mathematics, Language Arts, Science, and Social Studies

Subject	Matching Item

Mathematics	Match each item listed on the left with the numbered item on the right that best describes it.
	A. 0.006 = ___ 1. Nine thousand and one-tenth
	B. 2.3 = ___ 2. Six-thousandths
	C. 9000.10 = ___ 3. Six thousand
	D. 62.75 = ___ 4. Nine hundred
	                        5. Two and three-tenths
	                        6. Sixty-two and seventy-five–hundredths

Language arts	Match the following phrases with the literary techniques they exhibit.
	A. This backpack weighs a ton. ___
	B. She told Tommy about the tanks taking over Tamaroon. ___
	C. His eyes were as blue as the Sea of Cortez. ___
	D. Cats say "meow" while dogs say "woof." ___
	   1. Onomatopoeia 5. Alliteration
	   2. Hyperbole 6. Iambic pentameter
	   3. Metaphor 7. Simile
	   4. Extended metaphor 8. Assonance

Subject	Matching Item
Science	Match each part of the human brain to its basic function. 1. Frontal lobe ___ 2. Occipital lobe ___ 3. Temporal lobe ___ 4. Parietal lobe ___ A. Balance B. Memory C. Touch D. Pain E. Coordination of movements F. Vision
Social studies	Match the state listed on the left with its most famous landmark listed on the right. 1. District of Columbia ___ 2. Arizona ___ 3. South Dakota ___ 4. Texas ___ A. The Alamo B. The Pentagon C. The White House D. Mount Rushmore E. Everglades F. Grand Canyon

Table 4.3 Sample Alternative-Choice Items for Mathematics, Language Arts, Science, and Social Studies

Subject	Alternative-Choice Item
Mathematics	On a number line, a negative seven can be found: A. To the right of zero B. To the left of zero
Language arts	"Sally sold seashells" is an example of: A. Hyperbole B. Alliteration
Science	Photosynthesis is the process by which plants: A. Absorb nutrition B. Reproduce
Social studies	Entering into a new country with the intention of making it your home is called: A. Emigration B. Immigration

True/False

True/false items require students to determine if a statement is accurate or inaccurate (true or false). Table 4.4 (page 62) contains sample true/false items for mathematics, language arts, science, and social studies.

Multiple Response

Multiple-response items are like multiple-choice items. However, more than one of the alternatives can be correct. Table 4.5 (page 62) contains sample multiple-response items for mathematics, language arts, science, and social studies.

Table 4.4 Sample True/False Items for Mathematics, Language Arts, Science, and Social Studies

Subject	True/False Item
Mathematics	_____ The intersection of any two lines produces four 45-degree angles.
Language arts	_____ Quotation marks are used at the end of statements that are questions.
Science	_____ An atom is made up of a nucleus and its surrounding protons.
Social studies	_____ In medieval times, the Knights Templar was a holy order of knights pledged to minister to the sick and protect the holy places.

Table 4.5 Sample Multiple-Response Items for Mathematics, Language Arts, Science, and Social Studies

Subject	Multiple-Response Item
Mathematics	Put a check next to shapes for which you can find the volume. ___ Circle ___ Cube ___ Square ___ Sphere ___ Octagon ___ Prism
Language arts	Which of the following words show personal possession correctly? A. Margare'ts B. Rudy's C. Caroline's D. Erinns E. Hers F. Their G. Them
Science	Which of the following is an example of observation? A. We believe the parrots will perform better than the crows in self-recognition tests. B. Wolves run in packs. C. While watching people in the park, it appeared as though both adults and children were more friendly with people who were thin than with people who were overweight. D. We can conclude from these results that younger people tend to live in cities while older people tend to live in more rural areas. E. Between 7:00 and 8:00 a.m. on a particular day, 73 out of all of the people who ordered coffee in a particular coffee shop ordered some form of latte. G. None of the above statements are observations.
Social studies	Place a check in front of all occupations that can be found in the judicial branch. ___ President of the United States ___ Senator ___ Supreme Court justice ___ Secretary of State ___ Governor

Fill In the Blank

Fill-in-the-blank items require students to provide a response that fits into a specific phrase or sentence. Since these items do not require students to select a response, they are technically not selected-response items. They are better classified as "completion items," but they do require only one correct response. Consequently, they are similar to the other items in this section. Table 4.6 contains sample fill-in-the-blank items for mathematics, language arts, science, and social studies.

Table 4.6 Sample Fill-In-the-Blank Items for Mathematics, Language Arts, Science, and Social Studies

Subject	Fill-In-the-Blank Item
Mathematics	A fraction in which the numerator is greater than the denominator is a(n) _____ fraction.
Language arts	A poetic form employing three quatrains and a couplet (abab cdcd efef gg) is called a(n) _____.
Science	Animals that only eat vegetation are called _____, animals that only eat meat are called _____, and animals that eat both vegetation and meat are called _____.
Social studies	_____ was the first African American to hold an elected position.

Exercise 4.1 provides some practice in designing selected-response assessment items. (See page 77 for a reproducible of this exercise and page 142 for a reproducible answer sheet. Visit **marzanoresearch .com/classroomstrategiesthatwork** to download all the exercises and answers in this book.)

Exercise 4.1
Designing Selected-Response Assessment Items

The following content from various subject areas is presented along with a specific type of assessment item. Your task is to design the specified type of item for the content identified and then compare your answers with those provided on the corresponding answer sheet. To illustrate, assume you were given the following language arts content for the multiple-choice item type:

> **Language arts content**: A student should use one of the following strategies when trying to figure out the meaning of a word encountered while reading a text:
>
> 1. Look at the beginning letters and the ending letters of the word and ask yourself what word that begins and ends the same way would make sense.
>
> 2. Think of a word that would make sense in the sentence even if you know it is not the word you are trying to figure out.
>
> 3. Look up the unknown word in a dictionary.

You would then write a multiple-choice item that might look like the following:

> When you come to a word you don't know when reading a text, which of the following is not a good thing to do?
>
> A. Do not read on any further until you figure out the word.
>
> B. Look up the word in a dictionary.
>
> C. Try to think of any word that would make sense in the sentence in which the unknown word appears.
>
> D. Look at the first and last letters of the word and try to think of a familiar word that has those same beginning and ending letters.

Continued on next page →

1. **Multiple choice**: You are teaching a science unit on the animal kingdom, and you need to write a multiple-choice item for an upcoming assessment that addresses the following information:

   > There are five kingdoms: Animalia, Plantae, Protista, Fungi, and Monera. Humans are in Animalia.

2. **Matching**: You are teaching a social studies unit on World War II, and you need to write a matching item for an upcoming assessment that addresses the following information:

   > D day was on June 6, 1944; Truman took the office of the presidency on April 12, 1945; Hitler committed suicide on April 30, 1945; Hiroshima was bombed on August 6, 1945; and Nagasaki was bombed on August 9, 1945.

3. **Alternative choice**: You are teaching a mathematics unit on quadratic equations, and you need to write an alternative-choice item for an upcoming assessment that addresses the following information:

   > The formula for a quadratic equation is $ax^2 + bx + c = 0$.

4. **True/false**: You are teaching an art unit focusing on the performing arts, and you need to write a true/false item for an upcoming assessment that addresses the following information:

   > Improvisation is among the most effective techniques for improving stage presence.

5. **Multiple response**: You are teaching a physical education unit on basketball, and you need to write a multiple-response item for an upcoming assessment that addresses the following information:

   > The major fouls in basketball include personal fouls, charging, blocking, flagrant fouls, intentional fouls, and technical fouls.

6. **Fill in the blank**: You are teaching a health unit on nutrition, and you need to write a fill-in-the-blank item for an upcoming assessment that addresses the following information:

   > The human body uses ATP for sudden, powerful movements that require a few seconds of intense power, and the body uses three main sources for replenishing ATP once it has been expended: fat, carbohydrate, and protein.

Short Constructed-Response Items in Obtrusive Assessments

Short constructed-response items require students to construct a correct answer as opposed to recognizing one (as is the case for selected-response items). To this extent, they are more difficult than are selected-response items. While selected-response items are either correct or incorrect, short constructed-response items have shades that range from totally incorrect to totally correct. Of course, quantifying the intervals between totally correct and totally incorrect is the difficult part of scoring these items.

The following are short constructed-response items for mathematics, language arts, science, and social studies.

> *Mathematics*: Explain the steps necessary for finding the volume of a pyramid.

> *Language arts*: What persuasive techniques did you find in the reading passage? Describe whether they were effective or ineffective. Use specific examples in your answer.

> *Science*: Briefly explain the concept of circadian rhythm and why it is important.

> *Social studies*: Briefly explain the major accomplishments of Susan B. Anthony.

Designing and Scoring Assessments Using Selected-Response and Short Constructed-Response Items

One of the most common ways to design an obtrusive assessment is to combine selected-response items with short constructed-response items. Typically, selected-response items address the score 2.0

content while the short constructed-response items address the score 3.0 and 4.0 content. Table 4.7 illustrates this approach with an assessment for technology.

Table 4.7 An Assessment for Technology

Section I
1. Microsoft Word is best for graphic design projects.   True   False
2. If you want to make mathematical calculations or create data spreadsheets, _____ is one of the best programs to use.
3. The memory capacity of your computer is an example of hardware.   True   False
4. To connect to someone in another state for a video conference, you need:
A. An email address
B. An ID address
C. An IP address
D. None of the above
5. Which of the following is the larger unit of storage?
A. Gigabyte
B. Megabyte

Section II
6. Briefly discuss two things you can do to make sure the information you provide on the Internet will not be shared with anyone else. _____ _____ _____
7. If you make use of the spell check and grammar check features of Microsoft Word, do you still have to edit and proofread your own work? Why or why not? _____ _____ _____
8. Briefly describe the steps you would take to insert a three-dimensional shape such as a cylinder into a Microsoft Word document. _____ _____ _____

Section III
9. Of the virus protection software we have studied, pick the one you think has the most problems or disadvantages. Briefly describe what you see as being the major downfall(s) of this technology and suggest a better alternative. _____ _____ _____
10. Think about all of the ways you use the computer. If that technology vanished, how would you replace it? How do you think your life would change, and would it be a good change or a bad change? Why? _____ _____ _____

As shown in table 4.7, the first section of this assessment is composed of a series of selected-response items. These address the score 2.0 content. The second and third sections are composed of short constructed-response items. They address score 3.0 and 4.0 content, respectively. To score this assessment, a teacher would examine the pattern of responses as described in chapter 3. For example, assume that a particular student answered all five of the selected-response items correctly in section I. This would be an indication that the student has demonstrated at least score 2.0 competence. Again, selected-response items are easy to score. They are either correct or incorrect. This is not the case with short constructed-response items. They require the teacher's judgment, meaning that he or she must develop a scheme to keep track of how well students responded to short constructed-response items. For example, consider the following coding scheme:

C = Totally correct

I = Incorrect

P = Partially correct

Using this scheme, the teacher would code the student's response to each item as C, I, or P. Another coding scheme is:

C = Totally correct

I = Incorrect

LP = Low partial credit

HP = High partial credit

After coding each item, the teacher would examine the pattern of responses to assign a score on the scale. For example, assume that a student exhibited the pattern of responses depicted in table 4.8 for the ten-item assessment shown in table 4.7.

Table 4.8 Pattern of Responses for a Particular Student

Section	Item	Item Code	Score Value
I	1	C	2.0
	2	C	2.0
	3	C	2.0
	4	C	2.0
	5	C	2.0
II	6	HP	3.0
	7	C	3.0
	8	LP	3.0
III	9	I	4.0
	10	I	4.0

Clearly, the student depicted in table 4.8 has achieved at least score 2.0 status, since the items that pertain to that score value (section I) were answered correctly. Also, it is clear the student has not achieved score 4.0 status, since none of the score 4.0 items (section III) were answered correctly. The issue, then, is to determine where the student falls between score values 2.0 and 3.0. The student has answered one of the score 3.0 items totally correctly (item 7), one score 3.0 item with a code of low partial credit (item 8), and one score 3.0 item with a code of high partial credit (item 6). Given this pattern, the teacher would have to make a judgment as to the appropriate scale score. If half-point intervals were being used, the judgment would probably be fairly straightforward—the student would receive a score of 2.5. If the teacher were using a scale that employed one-third intervals, then the teacher would have to determine if the most appropriate score for the student would be 2.33 (indicating low partial knowledge of score 3.0 content) or 2.67 (indicating high partial knowledge of score 3.0 content). Given the pattern depicted in table 4.8 for the score 3.0 items, it would be logical to assign a score of 2.67.

On occasion, a student exhibits an uneven pattern of responses on a particular assessment. To illustrate, consider table 4.9.

Table 4.9 Uneven Pattern of Responses

Section	Item	Item Code	Score Value
I	1	C	2.0
	2	I	2.0
	3	C	2.0
	4	I	2.0
	5	C	2.0
II	6	C	3.0
	7	HP	3.0
	8	C	3.0
III	9	I	4.0
	10	I	4.0

In table 4.9, the student has answered all of the score 3.0 items correctly or with high partial credit. This indicates a score of 2.5 (if a half-point scale is being used) or a score of 2.67 (if a scale with one-third intervals is being used). However, the student has incorrectly answered two of the five score 2.0 items. Logically, such a pattern should not occur. Unfortunately, in the real world of classroom assessment, such patterns do occur. They occur in the world of state testing and standardized testing as well. Among test publishers, a pattern like this is referred to as an "aberrant pattern." Each year, test publishers carefully examine response patterns in their tests to identify and correct "aberrant items." They might drop items from the list, change items, or reclassify items.

An aberrant pattern can occur for a number of reasons, including the following:

- The items written for a particular score value were flawed in some way.

- Students put effort into answering some items but not others.

- The teacher's evaluation of student responses was inaccurate.

A teacher can do many things to reconcile the issue of aberrant patterns of response, including the following:

- Ignoring items that appear to be aberrant

- Meeting with individual students who display such patterns and asking them to reconcile the issues

- Reclassifying items at a higher or lower score value based on the responses of the entire class

(For a more detailed discussion, see Marzano, 2006.)

Extended Constructed-Response Items in Obtrusive Assessments

Extended constructed-response items require students to construct a detailed answer to a question or prompt. Most commonly, responses come in the form of essays. According to Mark Durm (1993), essays were one of the first forms of assessment used in public education. Marzano (2006, p. 80) provided the following example of an essay task that might be used to assess students using the scale presented in chapter 3.

> In 1858, Abraham Lincoln and Stephen Douglas debated during the campaign for the Senate seat representing the state of Illinois. You've been provided with a portion of what each of the debaters said. Read the comments of both Douglas and Lincoln and then respond to each of the following questions:
>
> 1. Douglas referred to a speech made by Lincoln in Springfield. What speech was Douglas referring to?
>
> 2. What did Douglas mean by the statement, "The Republic has existed from 1789 to this day divided into Free States and Slave States"?
>
> 3. In class we have talked about the generalization that for every defensible proposal, there is a defensible counterproposal. Explain how the Lincoln-Douglas debate exemplifies this generalization.
>
> 4. Identify a modern-day situation that reminds you of the Lincoln-Douglas debate. Explain how the debate and this situation are similar and different.

Excerpts from the Lincoln-Douglas debate accompanied this task, as shown in table 4.10.

Typically, essays are used to assess more complex content—score 3.0 and 4.0 content. This makes intuitive sense, as more complex information requires more detailed explanation. However, as shown in the essay prompt accompanied by table 4.10, essay tasks can be designed to address score 2.0 content also. Specifically, the first two questions embedded in the essay prompt deal with score 2.0 content—in this case, factual information about Lincoln's "House Divided" speech and the fact that up to the Civil War the republic of the United States was divided into two groups: states that had slaves and states that did not. If a student answered these parts of the essay prompt well, it would indicate that he or she had demonstrated at least score 2.0 competence. The third question embedded in the essay task addresses score 3.0 content in that it requires students to explain and exemplify a generalization presented in class. Finally, the fourth question embedded in the essay task addresses score 4.0 content in that it requires students to go above and beyond what was taught in class.

To score a student's essay, the teacher would code each section as described previously. The first two questions address score 2.0 content. If the student answered these satisfactorily, the teacher would record a C (correct) for each of the two responses. This would indicate that the student had demonstrated at least score 2.0 status. The third question deals with score 3.0 content. Again, if the student answered this question satisfactorily, the teacher would code the response as C (correct). This would indicate that the student had achieved at least score 3.0 status. Question 4 addresses score 4.0 content. If the student answered parts of this question satisfactorily, the teacher would code the response P (partial). Looking over the pattern of responses, the teacher would assign an overall score of 3.5.

Table 4.10 Excerpts From the Lincoln-Douglas Debate

Stephen A. Douglas
Mr. Lincoln tells you, in his speech made at Springfield, before the Convention which gave him his unanimous nomination, that:

"A house divided against itself cannot stand."

"I believe this government cannot endure permanently, half slave and half free."

"I do not expect the Union to be dissolved, I don't expect the house to fall; but I do think it will cease to be divided."

"It will become all one thing or all the other."

That is the fundamental principle on which he sets his campaign. Well, I do not suppose that you will believe one word of it when you come to examine it carefully, and see its consequences. Although the Republic has existed from 1789 to this day, divided into Free States and Slave States, yet we are told that in the future it cannot endure unless they shall become all free or all slave. For that reason he says ...

Abraham Lincoln
Judge Douglas made two points upon my recent speech at Springfield. He says they are to be the issue of my campaign. The first one of these points he bases upon the language in a speech which I delivered at Springfield which I believe I can quote correctly from memory. I said there that "we are now far into the fifth year since a policy was instituted for the avowed object, and with the confident purpose, of putting an end to slavery agitation; under the operation of that policy, that agitation has not only not ceased, but it has constantly augmented." "I believe it will not cease until a crisis shall have been reached and passed. 'A house divided against itself cannot stand.' I believe this Government cannot endure permanently half slave and half free." "I do not expect the Union to be dissolved"—I am quoting from my speech—"I do not expect the house to fall, but do expect it will cease to be divided. It will become one thing or the other. Either the opponents of slavery will arrest the spread of it and place it where the public mind shall rest, in the belief that it is in the course of ultimate extinction, or its advocates will push forward until it shall become alike lawful in all states, North as well as South."...

Source: Baker, Aschbacher, Niemi, & Sato (1992, pp. 19–22).

Another example of an essay task that deals with score 2.0, 3.0, and 4.0 content follows. The example is from art.

> Read the passage above and study the picture provided. Then answer the following questions:
>
> A. Who is the artist this passage is about, and what medium is he or she famous for?
>
> B. In what country and during what time period was this artist working?
>
> C. What were the unique elements of the artist's work, and how did people initially react?
>
> D. Compare this artist's work to one of the other artists we have studied. Who do you think is the superior artist and why?

Again, notice that this one essay prompt addresses score 2.0, 3.0, and 4.0 content. Items A and B address factual information (score 2.0 content). Item C requires students to describe the defining characteristics of the artist's work (score 3.0 content). Item D requires students to go beyond analysis of the artist's work and compare it with that of other artists (score 4.0 content).

Oral Responses in Obtrusive Assessments

Most of what can be assessed through the medium of written response can also be assessed using oral responses. Many times, though, oral responses are used to provide instructional feedback as opposed to formative scores. This is particularly true with short oral responses. We discussed this briefly in chapter 2.

To illustrate again, a teacher might prepare a series of true/false and multiple-choice items to ask students while he or she is presenting new content. Periodically during the presentation, the teacher might display one of the questions on a PowerPoint slide and ask students to respond orally. Assume the first question is a multiple-choice item with *a*, *b*, *c*, and *d* options—*d* being the correct response. A number of students might raise their hands, signaling that they know the correct answer. The teacher would call on one student, who says the answer is *a*. Instead of acknowledging whether the answer is correct or incorrect, the teacher would ask the student to explain why he or she thinks the answer is correct. The teacher would then call on another student, who believes the correct answer is a response other than *a*. Again, the student would be asked to explain his or her answer. The teacher would keep asking for student responses, eventually disclosing the correct answer. Student responses would not be scored or recorded.

As we saw in chapter 2, when assessments are not scored or recorded, they are referred to as instructional feedback and help both students and teachers understand what is clear and not clear about the content. As this example illustrates, short oral responses are a perfect vehicle for instructional feedback. Oral responses typically take one of two forms when they are used to generate formative scores: formal oral reports or probing interviews.

Formal Oral Reports

Oral reports have been used for years. They can be likened to essays in that students develop multiple drafts before the final product is presented. Additionally, there are certain expectations about how they are to be delivered, just as there are expectations about how essays are to be written and formatted. To illustrate a task that involves an oral report, consider the following example from language arts:

> We have been studying poets and prose writers of the Beat Generation. Choose one of the writers we have studied, and conduct independent research to answer the following questions in an oral report that is 10 to 15 minutes in length.
>
> A.   Is the writer you chose known as a poet or a prose writer, and what is most widely considered his or her best work?
>
> B.   Choose two defining stylistic or thematic characteristics of the Beat Generation, and describe how and where those characteristics appear in the work of your chosen writer. Use specific examples.
>
> C.   Are there any defining stylistic or thematic characteristics of your chosen writer's work that do not fit the traditional boundaries of the Beat Generation? Describe them using specific examples.
>
> D.   How do you think this writer's work has influenced today's artistic or pop culture? Discuss specific examples.

Notice that the directions to the oral report specify content that must be addressed by students. Items A and B deal with score 2.0 content, item C deals with score 3.0 content, and item D deals with score 4.0 content. With the aid of a well-written scale, a teacher can assign scores that represent all levels of the content embedded in the task.

Probing Discussions

Probing discussions are one of the most powerful forms of oral assessment. The teacher meets one-on-one with a particular student and asks him or her to explain or demonstrate something. For example, during a unit on relationships found in nature, a middle school science teacher might sit next to a student and ask her to explain the similarities and differences between mutualism, symbiosis, and commensalism. As the student explains these concepts, the teacher would ask probing questions that help to clarify what she knows and does not know. The scale that had been designed for this content would guide the teacher as to the types of questions he should ask to determine the scale score that most accurately represents the student's status at that point in time.

As another example, consider a primary teacher who has presented students with a strategy for previewing a book before reading it. That strategy might include the following:

- Looking at the cover and asking what the book might be about

- Looking through the pictures

- Asking questions that you would like to answer while reading the book

After presenting this strategy to students and allowing them to practice it, the teacher sits next to a particular student and asks him to use the previewing strategy with a book of his choice. As the student uses the strategy, the teacher asks him why he is doing certain things. The scale created specifically for this reading strategy guides the teacher in assigning a score based on the student's responses. Additional examples of probing discussions follow.

Social studies: A teacher invites a student into a discussion when studying the Panama Canal. She asks probing questions designed to find out if the student knows basic facts about the canal, such as how long it is, when it was finished, and what it is primarily used for today (score 2.0 content). She then asks the student to discuss the primary reasons for building the canal, and the major difficulties encountered during its construction (score 3.0 content). Finally, she asks the student to compare the Panama Canal project to a project on a similar scale (score 4.0 content).

Science: During a unit on the applications of Newton's laws of motion, a teacher invites a particular student into a discussion. He begins by asking the student to state the three laws in order (score 2.0 content). Next, he asks the student to describe a simple scenario that demonstrates one or more of the laws in action (score 3.0 content). Finally, he asks the student if he can think of any situation (such as zero gravity) in which those laws might be untrue (score 4.0 content).

Mathematics: During a unit on data analysis, a teacher invites a student to discuss a sample data chart. She asks the student to name the chart and give a general description of the kind of data it represents (score 2.0 content). She then asks the student to discuss the data displayed in a real-world context (score 3.0 content). Finally, she asks the student to consider another way in which the same data might be displayed and discuss whether or not the alternative way would be better (score 4.0 content).

Demonstrations in Obtrusive Assessments

Demonstrations are typically used with skills, strategies, or processes. Every subject area contains content that lends itself to demonstrations, though some subject areas emphasize skills, strategies, and processes more than others. Table 4.11 lists content from a number of subject areas that might readily be assessed through demonstration.

Table 4.11 Subject-Area Content for Demonstrations

Subject Area	Content That Can Be Assessed Through Demonstration
Language arts	• Using persuasive techniques in a composition • Using a literary device in a creative composition
Mathematics	• Computations of measures of central tendency • Analysis of data displays • Measurement of length, weight, and temperature
Science	• Hypothesis formulation and testing • Making relevant observations
Social studies	• Using a map's legend to gather information
Physical education	• Coordinating hand- and footwork during a game • Demonstrating teamwork during a game
Art	• Creating a dramatic character • Mixing and using color
Technology	• Creating a data display in Excel • Using spell check and grammar check

Demonstration tasks are relatively easy to construct. The teacher simply asks students to perform the skills, strategies, or processes. For example, a technology teacher might ask a student to demonstrate the proper use of spell check and grammar check. A physical education teacher might ask a student to play a few minutes of basketball, demonstrating the teamwork strategies that have been addressed in class.

In a situation where the skill, strategy, or process is mostly mental (as opposed to physical), the teacher might have to ask students to explain what they are thinking, or "think aloud" as they execute a skill, strategy, or process. For example, a language arts teacher asks a student to write a few sentences in which a specific literary device is used. As the student is doing so or when he has completed the set of sentences, the teacher asks him to explain his thinking while constructing the sentences. Demonstration tasks have the same basic characteristics as probing discussions (see page 71) when students are asked to "think aloud" as they use a skill, strategy, or process.

As in all situations, an assessment will be more or less easy to score depending on the specificity of the scale that has been constructed. The scales constructed for demonstrations must explicitly contain the expected behaviors for score 2.0, 3.0, and 4.0 content. Table 4.12 depicts a scale for hitting a softball.

Table 4.12 Hitting a Softball

Score 4.0	Students will be able to adapt their swings to differing speeds of a pitch.
Score 3.5	In addition to score 3.0 performance, partial success at score 4.0 content
Score 3.0	Students will begin hip rotation when the ball is about halfway to the plate, keep their eyes on the ball, and swing without dropping the back elbow.
Score 2.5	No major errors or omissions regarding score 2.0 content, and partial success at score 3.0 content
Score 2.0	Students will be able to use a stance in which feet are about shoulder width apart, back elbow is up, and bat is perpendicular to the ground.
Score 1.5	Partial success at score 2.0 content, but major errors or omissions regarding score 3.0 content
Score 1.0	With help, partial success at score 2.0 content and score 3.0 content
Score 0.5	With help, partial success at score 2.0 content, but not at score 3.0 content
Score 0.0	Even with help, no success

Notice that in table 4.12, specific behaviors are described for score 2.0, 3.0, and 4.0. With these behaviors clearly articulated on the scale, scoring a student's demonstration should be fairly straightforward.

Exercise 4.2 provides some practice in designing extended constructed-response and demonstration tasks. (See page 79 for a reproducible of this exercise and page 144 for a reproducible answer sheet. Visit **marzanoresearch.com/classroomstrategiesthatwork** to download all the exercises and answers in this book.)

Exercise 4.2
Designing Extended Constructed-Response and Demonstration Tasks

Following are target learning goals from three different subject areas. Select one of these subject areas and, in the space provided, generate an example of an extended constructed-response (essay) task or a demonstration task you might use as an assessment for that content. For example, if you select the content identified for science, your job would be to decide whether an essay task or a demonstration task would be more appropriate for the learning goal and then write an assessment item accordingly. For each task, make sure your directions require students to demonstrate their understanding of the target learning goal (score 3.0 content), simpler content (score 2.0 content), and more complex content (score 4.0 content). Compare your answers with those provided on the corresponding answer sheet when you are finished.

Mathematics learning goal: Students will be able to make conversions between standard and nonstandard measurement systems.

Science learning goal: Students will be able to discuss the water cycle and each of its stages.

Social studies learning goal: Students will be able to describe the events in a key battle from the Civil War and explain why either the Union or the Confederacy was the victor.

Essay task: _____

_____

Demonstration task: _____

_____

Unobtrusive Assessments

As is the case with demonstrations, unobtrusive assessments are most easily applied to skills, strategies, and processes. This is because skills, strategies, and processes usually involve doing something that is observable. Thus, a teacher might "catch" a student performing a skill, strategy, or process in a natural setting. For example, consider the physical skill of hitting a softball. A physical education teacher might observe a student hitting a softball during recess and record this observation as a formative score. Similarly, an art teacher might observe a student executing a particular type of brushstroke in class and record this observation as a formative score.

Both of the preceding examples involve physical procedures, which are amenable to unobtrusive assessments because they are easily observed. Mental procedures are more difficult to observe. For example, assume that a teacher has taught a specific decision-making strategy. It would be difficult to unobtrusively observe a student executing the steps of decision making. Typically, a teacher would have to ask questions of the student to determine his or her mental process. In effect, this would render the assessment a type of probing discussion. Examples of unobtrusive assessments from various subject areas follow.

> *Language arts*: A teacher notices during a presentation by a guest speaker that a student is using the recently taught note-taking skills to jot down the speaker's main ideas. He is jotting down questions as well. The teacher recognizes this as a score 3.0 demonstration of one of their learning goals and records the score in her gradebook.

> *Mathematics*: An elementary teacher is monitoring the lunch line when he notices one of his students in line waiting to pay for her lunch. The teacher sees the student look at the price tags of three things she will be purchasing and take out the correct amount of money from her school bag. He recognizes this as a score 3.0 demonstration of a learning goal on mental computation and records the score in his gradebook after the lunch period is over.

> *Science*: While students are performing experiments independently, the teacher takes note of which students are properly using the safety equipment set at each of their work stations. She records these scores in her gradebook for the learning goal regarding following safety procedures.

> *Social studies*: A social studies teacher who volunteers his time as a debate coach notices that one of his students chooses a topic regarding a current event. He finds that the student delivers accurate and relevant information on her topic during the debate and records a score 3.0 in his gradebook for a learning goal on current events.

> *Physical education*: During Field Day, a teacher notices a student playing the egg-toss game with a friend. He demonstrates correct underhand throwing technique, and his aim is much better than what the teacher has seen from him in class. The teacher records the improved score in her gradebook.

> *Art*: A choir teacher notices two of his students practicing in the music room after school with their band. One begins to play a tune on the guitar, and the other listens for a moment and joins in on the bass. The teacher sees this as a score 3.0 demonstration for a learning goal regarding improvisation and records the score for both students.

> *Technology*: During a PowerPoint presentation on a chosen topic, the teacher notices a student having trouble with his slides. She watches as the student troubleshoots the problem

successfully and moves on with the presentation. The teacher recognizes this as a score 4.0 demonstration for a learning goal regarding the fluent use of a software program and records the score in her gradebook.

Student-Generated Assessments

Perhaps the most powerful and underutilized type of assessment is student-generated assessment. As the name indicates, with this type of assessment, students propose tasks that will demonstrate their knowledge of a specific topic. Usually, students use student-generated assessments to move from one level on the scale to the next. To illustrate, an elementary language arts student proposes that he submit the following assignment as an indication that he has moved from a score 2.0 to 3.0 on a scale for the topic of reading comprehension.

> I have a score of 2.0 in the learning goal about literary elements right now, and I want to move up to a score of 3.0. I think I will select a story we have read and show how changing one element would influence other elements. For example, I will explain how changing just one character trait would influence the story's message and how changing the setting could influence the plot. By showing how all the elements work together, I think I can prove I understand the goal on literary elements at score 3.0.

In a middle school science class, a student proposes the following task as an indication that she has moved from a score 3.0 to 4.0 on a scale regarding the topic of the geosphere.

> Right now I have a 3.0 for the learning goal about the rocks and minerals in a geosphere. I think I can prove I deserve a 4.0 by showing how the "systems of the earth" we have studied interact as part of a huge system. I will show how changes in the *hydrosphere* (that we learned about last semester) can influence the processes of the *geosphere*—especially the rock cycle that we have been studying.

The following are examples from other subject areas:

Language arts: To demonstrate score 3.0 competence for a learning goal regarding spelling, an elementary student proposes he take a short verbal spelling test with the teacher after school.

Mathematics: To demonstrate score 3.0 competence in graphing linear equations, a student proposes she solve and graph the equations in the practice section of the textbook.

Science: A student who wants to demonstrate score 4.0 competence in physical science for a learning goal involving combustibility proposes he bring in a short video clip of the *Hindenburg* his dad has and explain step-by-step what caused the explosion.

Social studies: To demonstrate score 3.0 competence in U.S. history for a learning goal regarding the civil rights movement, a student proposes she create a timeline that includes the major relevant events of that time. Furthermore, she thinks she can demonstrate score 4.0 competence if she sits down with the teacher after creating the timeline to discuss how one event affected another and how this cause-and-effect chain created the momentum for a movement.

Physical education: A student brings his teacher a video his mother took of his football game the past weekend. He wants to show the teacher that the video displays his improved sportsmanship, a learning goal the student has struggled with all year. He thinks that if the teacher sees him encouraging his teammates when the team has fallen behind and congratulating the players on the other team when they win, the teacher will see this as demonstrating score 3.0 competence for that learning goal.

Art: A student shows her art teacher a sketchbook she has been keeping independently, because she thinks her drawings of the boats on the lake near her family's summer house demonstrate score 3.0 competence for a learning goal regarding perspective.

Technology: A student who wants to demonstrate score 3.0 competence for a learning goal regarding fluency with a software program proposes that he bring in a photo he has manipulated using Photoshop and explain step-by-step how he manipulated the photo.

Exercise 4.3 provides some review questions for this chapter. (See page 80 for a reproducible of this exercise and page 145 for a reproducible answer sheet. Visit **marzanoresearch.com/classroomstrat egiesthatwork** to download all the exercises and answers in this book.)

Exercise 4.3
Review Questions

> The following questions address much of the important content presented in this chapter. Answer each one and then compare your answers with those provided on the corresponding answer sheet.
>
> 1. How are selected-response items and short constructed-response items typically used to design a paper/pencil test that addresses score 2.0, 3.0, and 4.0 content?
> 2. Explain what you would do if a student demonstrated an aberrant pattern of responses in an assessment designed to address score 2.0, 3.0, and 4.0 content.
> 3. Explain why a well-constructed scale is critical to scoring a demonstration and unobtrusive observations.

Summary

This chapter began by addressing how to design obtrusive assessments by using combinations of selected-response items, short constructed-response items, and extended-response items. Selected-response items usually address score 2.0 content as they require students to recognize correct information, and they include the following types: multiple-choice items, matching items, alternative-choice items, true/false items, multiple-response items, and fill-in-the-blank items. Short constructed-response items usually address score 3.0 and 4.0 content and require students to recall information presented and to construct a response independently. Extended-response items usually come in the form of essays and can address score 2.0, 3.0, and 4.0 content. Because short- and extended-response items allow for partial credit, a coding scheme for recording students' precise patterns of response was presented. Oral reports, probing discussions, and demonstrations can be used in obtrusive assessments as well. Unobtrusive assessments are most easily applied to skills, strategies, and processes, and students who wish to move from one level on the scale to the next usually employ student-generated assessments.

Exercise 4.1

Designing Selected-Response Assessment Items

The following content from various subject areas is presented along with a specific type of assessment item. Your task is to design the specified type of item for the content identified and then compare your answers with those provided on the corresponding answer sheet. To illustrate, assume you were given the following language arts content for the multiple-choice item type:

Language arts content: A student should use one of the following strategies when trying to figure out the meaning of a word encountered while reading a text:

1. Look at the beginning letters and the ending letters of the word and ask yourself what word that begins and ends the same way would make sense.

2. Think of a word that would make sense in the sentence even if you know it is not the word you are trying to figure out.

3. Look up the unknown word in a dictionary.

You would then write a multiple-choice item that might look like the following:

When you come to a word you don't know when reading a text, which of the following is not a good thing to do?

A. Do not read on any further until you figure out the word.

B. Look up the word in a dictionary.

C. Try to think of any word that would make sense in the sentence in which the unknown word appears.

D. Look at the first and last letters of the word and try to think of a familiar word that has those same beginning and ending letters.

1. **Multiple choice**: You are teaching a science unit on the animal kingdom, and you need to write a multiple-choice item for an upcoming assessment that addresses the following information:

There are five kingdoms: Animalia, Plantae, Protista, Fungi, and Monera. Humans are in Animalia.

1 of 2

2. **Matching:** You are teaching a social studies unit on World War II, and you need to write a matching item for an upcoming assessment that addresses the following information:

> D day was on June 6, 1944; Truman took the office of the presidency on April 12, 1945; Hitler committed suicide on April 30, 1945; Hiroshima was bombed on August 6, 1945; and Nagasaki was bombed on August 9, 1945.

3. **Alternative choice:** You are teaching a mathematics unit on quadratic equations, and you need to write an alternative-choice item for an upcoming assessment that addresses the following information:

> The formula for a quadratic equation is $ax^2 + bx + c = 0$.

4. **True/false:** You are teaching an art unit focusing on the performing arts, and you need to write a true/false item for an upcoming assessment that addresses the following information:

> Improvisation is among the most effective techniques for improving stage presence.

5. **Multiple response:** You are teaching a physical education unit on basketball, and you need to write a multiple-response item for an upcoming assessment that addresses the following information:

> The major fouls in basketball include personal fouls, charging, blocking, flagrant fouls, intentional fouls, and technical fouls.

6. **Fill in the blank:** You are teaching a health unit on nutrition, and you need to write a fill-in-the-blank item for an upcoming assessment that addresses the following information:

> The human body uses ATP for sudden, powerful movements that require a few seconds of intense power, and the body uses three main sources for replenishing ATP once it has been expended: fat, carbohydrate, and protein.

Formative Assessment and Standards-Based Grading • © 2010 Marzano Research Laboratory • marzanoresearch.com
Visit **marzanoresearch.com/classroomstrategiesthatwork** to download this page.

Exercise 4.2

Designing Extended Constructed-Response Tasks and Demonstration Tasks

Following are target learning goals from three different subject areas. Select one of these subject areas and, in the space provided, generate an example of an extended constructed-response (essay) task or a demonstration task you might use as an assessment for that content. For example, if you select the content identified for science, your job would be to decide whether an essay task or a demonstration task would be more appropriate for the learning goal and then write an assessment item accordingly. For each task, make sure your directions require students to demonstrate their understanding of the target learning goal (score 3.0 content), simpler content (score 2.0 content), and more complex content (score 4.0 content). Compare your answers with those provided on the corresponding answer sheet when you are finished.

Mathematics learning goal: Students will be able to make conversions between standard and nonstandard measurement systems.

Science learning goal: Students will be able to discuss the water cycle and each of its stages.

Social studies learning goal: Students will be able to describe the events in a key battle from the Civil War and explain why either the Union or the Confederacy was the victor.

Essay task: _____

_____

_____

_____

Demonstration task: _____

_____

_____

_____

Exercise 4.3

Review Questions

The following questions address much of the important content presented in this chapter. Answer each one and then compare your answers with those provided on the corresponding answer sheet.

1. How are selected-response items and short constructed-response items typically used to design a paper/pencil test that addresses score 2.0, 3.0, and 4.0 content?

2. Explain what you would do if a student demonstrated an aberrant pattern of responses in an assessment designed to address score 2.0, 3.0, and 4.0 content.

3. Explain why a well-constructed scale is critical to scoring a demonstration and unobtrusive observations.

Chapter 5

TRACKING STUDENT PROGRESS

In chapter 2, we saw that tracking student progress over time is one of the defining features of the process of formative assessment. This chapter describes four basic approaches to tracking student progress. Each has unique characteristics, and each has advantages and disadvantages. Whether a particular teacher uses one approach over the other is frequently a matter of style and philosophy. It is also a matter of the content that is being addressed. A teacher might use one approach within a particular unit because it lends itself to the content of that unit; he or she might use a different approach in another unit for the same reason.

Approach 1: Summative Score Assigned at the End of the Grading Period

One approach to tracking student progress begins with designing assessments that include all levels of the assessment scale from the very beginning. For example, a mathematics teacher working on a unit about proportions designs and administers assessments that contain items for score values 2.0, 3.0, and 4.0 from the scale regarding proportion. Right from the first assessment, students can obtain scores that represent the full range on the scale—on the first assessment, students can receive scores as low as 0.0 and as high as 4.0. Of course, at the beginning of a unit, many students will probably not be able to answer items at score 3.0 and 4.0 values because this content has not yet been taught. However, a number of students might be able to answer items at score value 2.0 because those items contain content that is part of the students' general background knowledge.

Throughout the unit, students would graph their progress using the relevant scales. This is depicted in figure 5.1 (page 82). The method of tracking student progress shown in figure 5.1 was introduced and discussed in chapter 2. In the example here, six scores have been recorded: the first on February 5, the second on February 12, and so on. The student's last score in the set was 3.0. The summative score for the student is 3.5. As discussed in chapter 2, the teacher used the six formative scores as well as information about the student he or she might have gleaned from instructional feedback to assign the summative score. *The average of the formative scores should not be used as the summative score, nor should the final score in the set of scores be automatically assigned as the summative score.* Certainly the student's final score in the set (column f) is a good candidate for the final score, particularly if the final formative score represents a final examination of some sort. In figure 5.1, that final score of 3.0 has been derived from a final examination. If the teacher believes this score is the most accurate representation of the student's true level of understanding or skill relative to the learning goal, it should be recorded as the summative score. This is not the case in figure 5.1. Even though the last formative score of 3.0 came from a final examination, the teacher decided that the student's summative score was 3.5. To make this determination, the teacher probably used information about the student gleaned from instructional feedback.

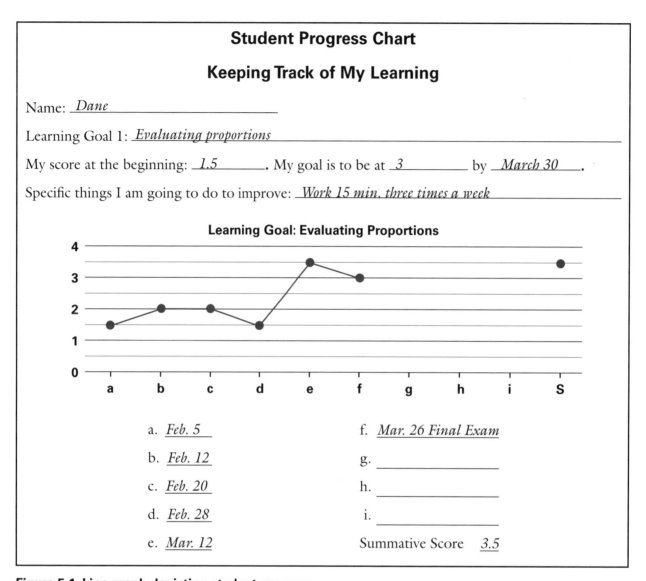

Figure 5.1 Line graph depicting student progress.

Students frequently exhibit variability in their formative scores for a given topic. Uneven patterns of formative scores require particular scrutiny by teachers. To illustrate, consider the following sequence of formative scores: 2.0, 3.0, 2.5, and 2.0. This sequence is not easy to interpret because it does not represent a clear upward trend. The student started with a score of 2.0 and ended with a score of 2.0. In between, the student received scores of 3.0 and 2.5. Obviously, there is no clear progression of learning. There are a number of reasons this type of pattern might occur. For example, the student might have gotten lucky when she received the scores of 3.0 and 2.5, and in this case, a score of 2.0 would probably be the best representation of her summative score. However, assume that the last score in the series (2.0) was simply a function of the student's not feeling well when that assessment was given. In this case, a score of 2.0 would be an underrepresentation of her final status.

The teacher has little option but to collect more information from the student when uneven patterns of scores occur. This might take the form of asking the student what she believes she deserves. If the student says she deserves a final score of 3.0, the teacher would invite her to suggest a student-generated assessment to verify the score 3.0 status. Alternatively, the teacher might engage her in a probing discussion to determine her true status. In summary, the operative behavior when a teacher observes an uneven pattern of formative scores is to gather more information about the student, using other forms of assessment.

Record Keeping

Record keeping in a system like this is much different from the traditional approach in which teachers simply record scores on tests without regard for what a particular test was designed to assess. In this system, the formative score derived from each assessment must be recorded along with the learning goal it is designed to assess. At the end of the chapter, we consider how to use electronic gradebooks to keep track of student progress. Here, we consider a paper/pencil approach. Table 5.1 (page 84) depicts a paper/pencil record-keeping system for approach 1 (a reproducible form for this approach can be found at the end of this chapter on page 101).

Each column in table 5.1 contains students' formative and summative scores for a single goal. The summative score is placed in the box at the bottom right of each cell. Notice that each column is assigned a letter—A through E. This indicates the learning goal to which the scores relate. An assessment key like that in table 5.2 (page 85) accompanies the gradebook sheets for each grading period. The assessment key allows a teacher to keep track of when assessments were administered and which learning goal(s) they addressed.

The top part of table 5.2 indicates that the first goal (goal A) requires the comparison of the earth's size and composition to the sizes and compositions of other planets. The bottom part of table 5.2 indicates that the first assessment was administered on January 5 and addressed learning goal A. The second assessment also addressed learning goal A and was administered on January 12. The third assessment was administered on January 15 and was also on goal A. Thus, in general, the first three entries for each student in column A represent these three assessments. Scores are entered into each cell from the top left to the bottom and then from the top right to the bottom if two columns of formative scores are required.

Consider the first row and column, which represent Katherine's formative scores on learning goal A. Notice that the third score has been circled. This indicates that it is not one of the teacher-designed assessments recorded in the assessment key. Instead, the score might have been derived from a probing discussion the teacher had with Katherine. At the end of the probing discussion, the teacher simply entered the score of 2.0 in the gradebook and put a circle around it to indicate that it was an assessment done with this student only.

Table 5.1 Gradesheet for Approach 1

	Goal A		Goal B	Goal C	Goal D	Goal E
Katherine	1.5 2.5 1.5 (2.0) 2.5					
Martin	2.5 Inc. 3.0 3.0					
Nam	3.0 3.0 3.5 3.5					
Betsy	0.5 2.0 4.0 4.0					
Alex	2.5 (2.5) 2.5 2.5 2.5					

Table 5.2 Assessment Key

Learning Goals
Goal A: The student will compare the size and composition of the earth to other planets.
Goal B: The student will describe matter by its physical and chemical properties.
Goal C: The student will describe how matter cycles through an ecosystem.
Goal D: The student will describe the influence of atmospheric conditions such as pressure and movement on weather patterns.

Assessments
Assessment 1:   Goal A: January 5
Assessment 2:   Goal A: January 12
Assessment 3:   Goal A: January 15
Assessment 4:

Notice the "incomplete" score recorded for Martin on learning goal A (second row, first column). Martin either missed or did not complete this assessment, but as opposed to recording a score of 0, the teacher simply noted the incomplete status of the assessment. A score of 0 is never recorded in the gradebook if a student has missed an assessment or has not completed an assignment. Many assessment researchers and theorists have addressed this issue in some depth (see Reeves, 2004; Guskey & Bailey, 2001). Briefly, no score should be entered into a gradebook that is not an estimate of a student's knowledge status for a particular topic at a particular point in time. Using the scale provided in chapter 3, it is theoretically possible for a student to receive a 0 on a particular assessment. This score indicates that even with help, the student cannot demonstrate partial knowledge of any content in the scale. Although 0 scores are rarely, if ever, assigned using the scale, it is possible at the beginning of a unit to assign a score of 0 to a student who knows nothing about the topic. Therefore, entering a 0 for not taking an assessment or as some type of punishment does not represent a student's true status and is *completely inappropriate*.

At the end of the grading period, the teacher examines the pattern of scores recorded in table 5.1 for each student and decides on a summative score. This summative score is recorded in the box at the bottom right of each box representing a learning goal for an individual student. Notice Betsy's final score (fourth row, first column). Even though Betsy began the unit with a very low score (0.5), she progressed rapidly, and at the end of the unit the teacher estimated her true score to be a 4.0. As explained previously, low scores at the beginning of a unit (even a score of 0) in no way limit the summative score a student can earn by the end of a unit.

In this approach, students can examine their individual progress on each learning goal. To do this, they simply compare where they began with where they ended. In figure 5.1 (page 82), Dane began with a score of 1.5 and ended with a score of 3.5—a gain of two full points.

Strengths and Weaknesses of Approach 1

Each of the four approaches addressed in this chapter has specific strengths and weaknesses. One of the strengths of this first approach is that students become aware of what is expected of them right from the very beginning of the unit. Because the first assessment contains items for scores 2.0, 3.0, and

4.0, students see exactly the type of content they are expected to master by the end of the unit. Another strength of this approach is that it is very easy to track knowledge gain. Each student has a clear beginning point and a clear ending point—the summative score.

The biggest weakness of this approach is that some students might be concerned when they do not receive high scores on the first few assessments in the unit. Currently, in many, if not most, classrooms across the country, students are assessed only on the content they have been taught. Thus, the traditional system fosters an expectation that something is amiss if students do not obtain high scores on every assessment. In this system, nothing is amiss if a student receives low scores on the first assessments. In fact, low initial scores are quite natural because much of the content on the scale has not been taught at the beginning of the unit.

Students and parents are typically concerned about low scores at the beginning of a unit because they are accustomed to teachers averaging scores to obtain a final score. As we have seen, this is not done in this approach (or in any other approach described in this chapter). Instead, final status is determined by looking at the trend over time and then estimating final true status in the form of a summative score. Once students and parents realize that low scores at the beginning of a unit will not be used punitively, they typically become comfortable with this approach.

Approach 2: Gradual Accumulation of a Summative Score

A defining characteristic of the second approach is that a *current* summative score is recorded throughout a unit or grading period as opposed to constructing a summative score at the end (as is the case with approach 1).

In this approach, the teacher typically begins by administering an assessment that addresses all score values of the scale. That is, the teacher designs an initial assessment that includes items for score 2.0, 3.0, and 4.0 content and administers it to the entire class, perhaps even before any instruction has begun. This, of course, is similar to approach 1.

In approach 2, however, the perspective changes dramatically after the initial assessment. From that point on, the teacher takes an individual approach to assessment, making heavy use of student-generated assessments. To increase a student's score on a scale, the teacher must be convinced that the student has demonstrated a commensurate increase in knowledge. Thus, there is typically a good deal of interaction between teacher and students. Students present evidence for moving to a higher score on the scale, and the teacher and students interact about that evidence to clarify the student's status.

To illustrate, assume that a student has said she will write a brief paper to demonstrate that she has attained score 3.0 status on a social studies learning goal. The teacher reads the student's paper, but he might also have a brief discussion with the student during which he seeks to clarify questions. This type of dialogue eliminates some of the error in measurement. As another example, assume that on the first assessment, a student received a score of 1.5 for a specific learning goal. A few days after that assessment, the teacher sits next to the student and engages in a probing discussion. As a result of that discussion, the teacher is convinced that the student has achieved at least a score 2.0 status and records the score in the gradebook. He also shades in the appropriate portion of the right-hand column in the student's cell of the gradesheet, as we will discuss under "Record Keeping."

In this approach, students can chart their progress as before. Figure 5.2 depicts the use of a bar graph as opposed to a line graph to chart student progress on a specific learning goal.

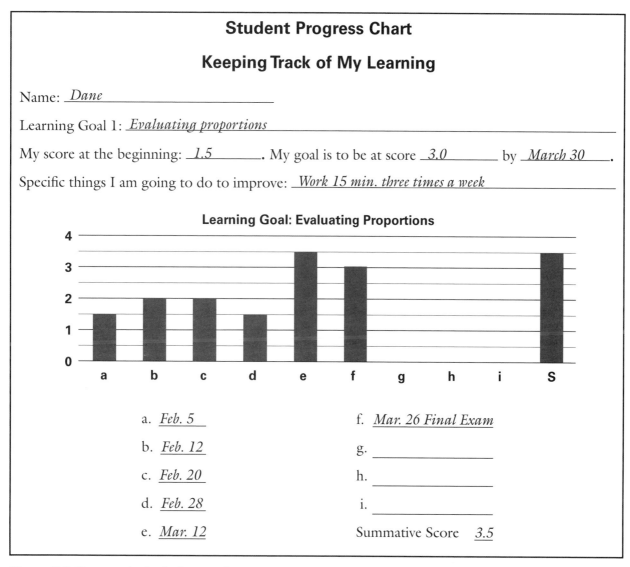

Figure 5.2 Bar graph depicting student progress.

Record Keeping

Record keeping in this system resembles the system in approach 1 with one notable exception. As mentioned previously, a current summative score is recorded for each student on each learning goal throughout the grading period. In the first approach, the teacher waits until the end of the grading period before entering a summative score.

The gradesheet used in this approach is depicted in table 5.3 (page 88; a reproducible form for this approach is presented at the end of this chapter on page 102).

While the gradesheet in table 5.3 is similar to the gradesheet in table 5.1 (page 84) in that each cell depicts scores for a specific student on a single learning goal, there is a column in table 5.3 at the right of each cell that has four boxes labeled 4.0, 3.0, 2.0, and 1.0, respectively. This column does not appear in the previous gradesheet. As formative scores are entered into the gradesheet, the teacher enters a "current" summative score by filling in the appropriate portion of the column on the right of each cell.

Table 5.3 Gradesheet for Approach 2

		Goal A		Goal B		Goal C		Goal D		Goal E
Chayla	1.5	4.0		4.0		4.0		4.0		4.0
	2.0	3.0		3.0		3.0		3.0		3.0
		2.0		2.0		2.0		2.0		2.0
		1.0		1.0		1.0		1.0		1.0
David	2.0	4.0		4.0		4.0		4.0		4.0
	2.5	3.0		3.0		3.0		3.0		3.0
	(3.5)	2.0		2.0		2.0		2.0		2.0
		1.0		1.0		1.0		1.0		1.0
Burke	3.0	4.0		4.0		4.0		4.0		4.0
	(3.0)	3.0		3.0		3.0		3.0		3.0
	3.5	2.0		2.0		2.0		2.0		2.0
		1.0		1.0		1.0		1.0		1.0
Eryn	2.5	4.0		4.0		4.0		4.0		4.0
	2.0	3.0		3.0		3.0		3.0		3.0
	(2.0)	2.0		2.0		2.0		2.0		2.0
		1.0		1.0		1.0		1.0		1.0
Alicia	3.0	4.0		4.0		4.0		4.0		4.0
	4.0	3.0		3.0		3.0		3.0		3.0
		2.0		2.0		2.0		2.0		2.0
		1.0		1.0		1.0		1.0		1.0

To illustrate, consider the first student, Chayla, and the first learning goal. Chayla has two scores: 1.5 and 2.0. The teacher has shaded in the column in the right-hand side of the cell up to the score of 2.0. This indicates that at this point in time, the teacher judges Chayla to be at score 2.0 status. Stated differently, if the teacher had to assign a summative score at this point in time, it would be a 2.0. Again, the teacher does not simply assume that the last formative score is the best representation of the student's current summative score. Rather, he or she uses all available information about the student, including that gleaned from instructional feedback, to shade in a current summative score.

Also consider David's scores in the second row. David has three scores: 2.0, 2.5, and 3.5. The circle around score 3.5 indicates that it was not one of the obtrusive assessments designed and administered by the teacher. This could have been a student-generated assessment proposed by David. Notice that the column in the right-hand side of the cell is filled in up to halfway through score 4.0. This indicates that David's current summative score is 3.5.

In approach 2, the teacher makes heavy use of student-generated assessments after the initial assessment. As formative scores are entered into the gradebook, the teacher uses this information as well as information gleaned from instructional feedback to assign current summative scores.

Strengths and Weaknesses of Approach 2

One of the strengths of the second approach is that it is individualized. After the initial assessment, each student is considered an independent case. Perhaps the biggest strength of this approach is that it puts students at the center of the assessment process because they are responsible for providing evidence of their progress.

The biggest weakness of this approach is that it is quite labor-intensive because the teacher must meet frequently with individual students to assess their progress.

Approach 3: The Whole Class Progresses as One

In the first two approaches, the focus is on individual students. In the third approach, the focus is on the entire class as a unit. That is, the whole class moves up the scale at approximately the same pace. Additionally, the teacher assesses the content for score values 2.0, 3.0, and 4.0 separately. To illustrate, assume that a teacher has developed a scale for a learning goal that is the focus of a unit. The first assessment he or she administers comes after the score 2.0 content has been presented in class and focuses on score 2.0 content only. The assessments for this level might employ selected-response items exclusively, as these types of items are typically used with score 2.0 content (see chapter 4). Of course, this is very different from approaches 1 and 2, both of which employ initial assessments that include items for all score values in the scale.

In the third approach, the teacher continues teaching and assessing score 2.0 content until the entire class (or close to it) has demonstrated mastery of the content. The teacher moves on to score 3.0 content when he or she is reasonably sure all students have reached or will eventually reach 2.0 status. These assessments might be quite different from the previous ones, as they address more complex content. As we saw in chapter 4, score 3.0 content is commonly assessed using constructed-response formats. Again, the teacher waits until the class as a whole has demonstrated mastery of the content, and then he or she moves on to score 4.0 content.

Record Keeping

In this approach, teachers employ one of the record-keeping schemes described in approach 1 or 2, and students still keep track of their progress on specific learning goals as depicted in figure 5.1 or 5.2 (pages 82, 87). Additionally, in approach 3, progress can be tracked for the entire class, as seen in figure 5.3 (page 90).

In figure 5.3, the percentage of students who have reached scores 2.0, 3.0, and 4.0 is depicted in three separate bars. The first bar represents the percentage of students who have mastered score 2.0 content, the second bar represents the percentage of students who have mastered score 3.0 content, and so on.

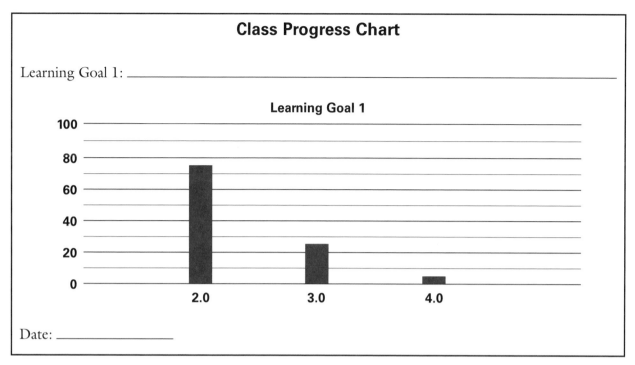

Figure 5.3 Bar graph depicting class progress.

Strengths and Weaknesses of Approach 3

The major strength of approach 3 is that it looks familiar to students and parents. Students tend to receive high scores on all assessments because they are assessed only on what has been taught. Although the failings of the 100-point scale were detailed in chapter 3, it can be used in approach 3 with some integrity. That is, when assessing score 2.0 content, a teacher might design assessments that employ the 100-point scale. A "cut score" would be established that represents satisfactory knowledge of the content at a specific score value. For example, for score 2.0 content, the teacher might determine that a score of 80 percent on a specific assessment indicates that students know the content well enough to start working on the score 3.0 content.

Because each assessment focuses on the content for a particular score value only, the differential weighting of items (discussed in chapter 3) is not as big an issue. The items on an assessment tend to be more alike because they all address the same level of content. Thus, the 100-point scale makes a little more sense in this system.

A big weakness of this approach is that it does not address individual student needs very well. This is because all students in the class move through the content at about the same pace. This might frustrate students at both ends of the knowledge continuum. That is, students who already know advanced content at the beginning of the unit might become frustrated because the class is moving too slowly. Conversely, students who have no previous understanding of the content prior to the unit might find the class is moving too rapidly. In this approach it is common for a teacher to move to the next level when the vast majority of students have reached a specific level. Thus, some students are always moving to the next level before they are ready.

Approach 4: Continual Improvement Throughout the Year

As its name implies, approach 4 allows students to increase their scores on any topic throughout the entire year. To illustrate how this works, assume that a fifth-grade language arts teacher has identified the following thirty learning goals for the year:

Language:

1. Students will use word roots and prefixes and suffixes to spell and decode unknown words.

2. Students will use context clues to decode the meaning of unknown words.

3. Students will use common punctuation marks such as commas, semicolons, colons, quotations marks, apostrophes, and parentheses correctly.

4. Students will describe slight differences in the meanings of related words.

5. Students will describe the meaning and effect of metaphors, similes, and hyperboles.

6. Students will appropriately use commonly misused verbs (for example, lay/lie).

Reading:

7. Students will describe both explicit and implicit themes.

8. Students will describe complex causal relationships.

9. Students will describe complex chronologies.

10. Students will make and defend predictions.

11. Students will describe the main idea of a composition and make predictions about its intended audience.

12. Students will identify persuasive techniques such as appeal to emotion, appeal to logic, and appeal to authority, and discuss their effectiveness in specific situations.

13. Students will identify errors in logic in persuasive compositions.

14. Students will compare and contrast different kinds of fiction and nonfiction (for example, novels versus short stories or biographies versus historical accounts).

15. Students will identify the defining aspects of poetry such as line breaks and linguistic rhythm.

Writing:

16. Students will use all tense forms correctly and consistently in writing and switch tense when necessary.

17. Students will choose an appropriate audience for a composition and maintain attention to it throughout a composition.

18. Students will write personal and business letters using specified formats.

19. Students will write expository compositions that focus on comparison/contrast.

20. Students will write narrative compositions that use consistent point of view.

21. Students will write narrative compositions with attention to forms of characterization such as dialogue and self-description.

22. Students will make a basic outline for a composition (for example, a chronological list of important events the student will discuss in a composition about an important person).

23. Students will use standard reference books and Internet search engines to gather relevant information for a composition.

24. Students will self-edit to correct misspellings and run-on sentences or sentence fragments and factual mistakes.

25. Students will edit for overall clarity.

Verbal communication:

26. Students will use active listening skills such as taking notes and asking clarifying questions.

27. Students will summarize the main points made by a speaker.

28. Students will deliver oral presentations with attention to enunciation, pace, and eye contact.

29. Students will describe the advantages and disadvantages of information delivered through mass media.

30. Students will compare and contrast different mass media (for example, television, Internet, radio, and magazines).

Scales would be constructed for each of these learning goals. Assume that during the first unit of instruction the teacher addresses the first two learning goals, assigning summative scores in accordance with approach 1 or 2. In the next unit, the teacher might address the next two learning goals—goals 3 and 4. However, during the second unit, students would have opportunities to work on the learning goals from the first unit in an effort to raise their scores. Of course, this would require setting aside time in class for students to work individually or in groups to improve their scores on previously addressed goals (for a discussion on how a class can be organized to support this effort, see *Designing and Teaching Learning Goals and Objectives*, Marzano, 2009).

Throughout the year, the teacher continues to present new learning goals in new units, gradually working through the thirty goals during the course of the year. However, at any point in time, students can raise their scores on previous learning goals. Most commonly, this is done through student-generated assessments. That is, students propose ways they can demonstrate a higher score on a particular learning goal. If the teacher judges the evidence the student provides as worthy of an increased score, then the student's score is changed. In other words, the summative scores recorded for the topics addressed during any unit can be continually updated throughout the year, hence the continual-improvement focus of this approach.

Record Keeping

In approach 4, students keep track of two types of progress, the first of which is their progress on individual learning goals as units are presented. This can be done using the record-keeping formats described in any of the previous approaches.

In addition to keeping track of progress on each learning goal, students keep track of the number of goals in which they have demonstrated "mastery." Typically, a score of 3.0 on the scale is considered mastery of the content. The expectation is that by the end of the year, all students will have a score of 3.0 or higher (scores 3.5 or 4.0) on each learning goal. Thus, the continual-improvement approach has a mastery orientation. Each student keeps track of his or her individual progress across all learning goals throughout the year with the intent of achieving a score of 3.0 on each one. Table 5.4 depicts a record-keeping form students might use (a reproducible version of this form is found at the end of this chapter on page 103).

Table 5.4 Continual Progress Report

	0.0	0.5	1.0	1.5	2.0	2.5	3.0	3.5	4.0
Goal 1: Students will use word roots and prefixes and suffixes to spell and decode unknown words.	▓	▓	▓	▓	▓				
Goal 2: Students will use context clues to decode the meaning of unknown words.	▓	▓	▓	▓	▓	▓			
Goal 3: Students will use common punctuation marks such as commas, semicolons, colons, quotations marks, apostrophes, and parentheses correctly.	▓	▓	▓	▓					
Goal 4: Students will describe slight differences in the meanings of related words.	▓	▓	▓	▓	▓	▓	▓		
Goal 5: Students will describe the meaning and effect of metaphors, similes, and hyperboles.	▓	▓	▓	▓	▓	▓			
Goal 6: Students will appropriately use commonly misused verbs (lay/lie).	▓	▓	▓	▓	▓				
Goal 7: Students will describe both explicit and implicit themes.	▓	▓	▓	▓	▓	▓	▓	▓	
Goal 8: Students will describe complex causal relationships.	▓	▓	▓	▓	▓	▓			
Goal 9: Students will describe complex chronologies.	▓	▓	▓	▓	▓				
Goal 10: Students will make and defend predictions.	▓	▓	▓	▓	▓	▓	▓		

Continued on next page →

Goal 11: Students will describe the main idea of a composition and make predictions about its intended audience.	■	■	■	■	■				
Goal 12: Students will identify persuasive techniques such as appeal to emotion, appeal to logic, and appeal to authority, and discuss their effectiveness in specific situations.	■	■	■	■	■	■	■		
Goal 13: Students will identify errors in logic in persuasive compositions.	■	■	■	■	■	■	■	■	
Goal 14: Students will compare and contrast different kinds of fiction and nonfiction (novels vs. short stories or biographies vs. historical accounts).	■	■	■	■	■	■			
Goal 15: Students will identify the defining aspects of poetry such as line breaks and linguistic rhythm.	■	■	■	■	■	■			
Goal 16: Students will use all tense forms correctly and consistently in writing and switch tense when necessary.	■	■	■	■	■	■			
Goal 17: Students will choose an appropriate audience for a composition and maintain attention to it throughout a composition.	■	■	■	■	■	■	■		
Goal 18: Students will write personal and business letters using specified formats.									
Goal 19: Students will write expository compositions that focus on comparison/contrast.									
Goal 20: Students will write narrative compositions that use consistent point of view.									
Goal 21: Students will write narrative compositions with attention to forms of characterization such as dialogue and self-description.									
Goal 22: Students will make a basic outline for a composition (chronological list of important events the student will discuss in a composition about an important person).									
Goal 23: Students will use standard reference books and Internet search engines to gather relevant information for a composition.									
Goal 24: Students will self-edit to correct misspellings and run-on sentences or sentence fragments and factual mistakes.									

Goal 25: Students will edit for overall clarity.									
Goal 26: Students will use active listening skills such as taking notes and asking clarifying questions.									
Goal 27: Students will summarize the main points made by a speaker.									
Goal 28: Students will deliver oral presentations with attention to enunciation, pace, and eye contact.									
Goal 29: Students will describe the advantages and disadvantages of information delivered through mass media.									
Goal 30: Students will compare and contrast different mass media (television, Internet, radio, and magazines).									

Notice that in table 5.4, each row represents a specific learning goal. Notice that the student has filled in current summative scores for seventeen of the thirty learning goals to be addressed throughout the school year. This table probably represents the student's status at the midpoint of the year. The remaining thirteen goals will be addressed the second half of the year. As new goals are addressed in class, students fill in their summative scores. The intent is that each student attains at least a score 3.0 on all learning goals by the end of the school year.

Finally, it is important to recognize that a teacher would probably not address the thirty learning goals in the lockstep fashion depicted in table 5.4. Rather, the teacher would probably address selected learning goals from language (goals 1–6), reading (goals 7–15), writing (goals 16–25), and verbal communication (goals 26–30) each quarter. For ease of discussion, we have represented the progression through the thirty learning goals in a linear manner.

Strengths and Weaknesses of Approach 4

The major strength of approach 4 is its focus on yearlong improvement. The intent is that every student attains a score of 3.0 or higher on *every* topic. Therefore, students can go back and enhance their knowledge of any goal that has been addressed throughout the entire year. As pointed out in *Designing and Teaching Learning Goals and Objectives* (Marzano, 2009), "Most state standards documents identify content that should be learned *by the end of the school year*" (p. 92). This statement directly implies that students should have opportunities throughout the year to raise their scores on any of the learning goals addressed. Approach 4 also allows a student to move through the content at his or her own pace because he or she may also work on topics that have not yet been explicitly addressed by the teacher.

In a system like this, students typically take more responsibility for their own learning. This stems directly from the fact that students have the flexibility to raise scores on any learning goal at any time during the school year. In effect, if students do not attain relatively high scores on the learning goals addressed during the year, they have little to blame but their own lack of initiative.

The main disadvantage of this approach is that it is highly labor-intensive because record keeping is cumulative throughout the entire year. Another possible disadvantage of this approach is that it is very different from the manner in which classrooms are currently configured. In the present system, once a topic has been taught, students have little or no opportunity to raise their scores. Thus, approach 4 is a dramatic shift from the current system and may take some acculturation. This noted, many students relish this shift, as it provides more opportunities to advance their learning and does not punish them for starting slowly.

Exercise 5.1 provides some practice in record keeping. (See page 99 for a reproducible of this exercise and page 146 for a reproducible answer sheet. Visit **marzanoresearch.com/classroomstrategies thatwork** to download all the exercises and answers in this book.)

Exercise 5.1
Record Keeping in the Four Approaches

> The following questions address much of the content presented thus far. Answer each one and then compare your answers with those provided on the corresponding answer sheet.
>
> 1. While using approach 1, a particular student exhibits the following pattern of formative scores for a particular learning goal: 2.0, 2.5, 3.0, 3.5, and 2.5. Describe how you would determine the student's summative score. Make sure to explain your reasoning.
> 2. Explain why the 100-point scale can be used with approach 3 but not with approach 1 or 2.
> 3. Explain why it is not a good idea to automatically use the last score in a set of formative scores as the summative score, even if the final score comes from a final examination.
> 4. Explain why it is inappropriate to enter a score of 0 if a student misses an assessment or does not complete an assignment.

Celebrating Current Status and Knowledge Gain

One of the major advantages of using the scale described in this book is that teachers and students can celebrate two types of achievement at any point in time—current status and knowledge gain. Current status refers to a student's score at the end of a particular interval of time—usually a quarter, trimester, or semester. Consequently, a teacher can acknowledge all of those students who have a score of 4.0 on a given learning goal, all of the students with a score of 3.5, and so on. In addition, the teacher can and should celebrate knowledge gain. Knowledge gain is the difference between a student's initial formative score and his or her score at the end of a quarter, trimester, or semester. For example, assume that for a specific learning goal, a student's initial formative score was 1.5. At the end of the quarter, the student's summative score is 2.5. The "gain" score for that student is 1.0.

The Role of Technology

Thus far, we have not considered the role of technology in keeping track of student progress. Obviously, record keeping is much easier if the teacher does not have to record students' scores by hand. One system that allows for easy entry of student scores and provides access to a variety of reports is the Pinnacle Suite available from GlobalScholar (see www.globalscholar.com). Formative scores for students are entered into the gradebook using a matrix like that in table 5.5.

Table 5.5 Pinnacle Suite View for Entering Scores on Assessments

Student Name	Assessment 1: Rights and Responsibilities	Assessment 2: Rights and Responsibilities	Assessment 3: The Constitution
Wally	2.5	2.0	2.0
Monique	2.0	2.0	3.0
Enrique	2.5	3.0	3.0
Jake	2.0	2.5	1.5
Olivia	3.0	3.0	3.0
Raymond	3.0	3.0	3.0
Indira	2.5	2.5	2.0
Esther	3.0	3.5	4.0
Nadya	1.5	2.0	2.5
June	3.5	3.5	3.0

Table 5.5 depicts formative scores for students. Each column represents a different assessment. The first column represents an assessment on a learning goal related to rights and responsibilities. The second column contains formative scores from a second assessment, also on this learning goal. The third column contains formative scores from a third assessment, but this one is on a learning goal related to the Constitution.

As the teacher develops assessments for learning goals, he or she simply enters students' scores in the next available column and indicates which goal a column represents. The technology then keeps track of the learning goal with which each column is associated, when assessments were administered, and each student's progress on each learning goal. To illustrate, consider figure 5.4.

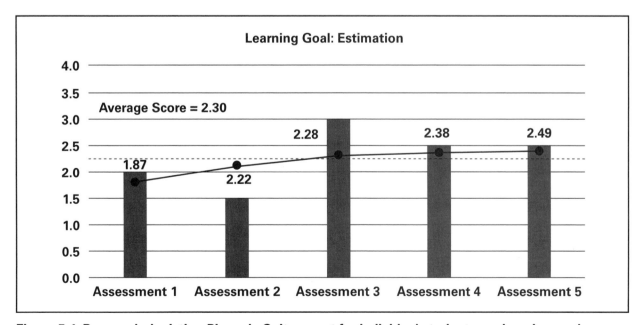

Figure 5.4 Bar graph depicting Pinnacle Suite report for individual student on a learning goal.

Figure 5.4 contains one of the many reports that can be generated for any student (or the entire class) at any point in time. In this case, the report tracks a specific student's progress on a specific learning goal. Notice that five bars are presented in figure 5.4. These represent five formative scores that have been collected on the student. The first formative score is 2.0; the last in the set is 2.5. Also note that the figure contains a trend line. This depicts the mathematical trend for the student's five formative scores. This is powerful information that can be used to construct a summative score for the student. For a detailed discussion of how this trend score and other useful scores are computed, see Marzano (2006).

Technology provides tools that allow teachers to easily enter formative scores for different learning goals throughout a grading period. These scores are analyzed in ways that generate a variety of reports for individual students, an entire class, a school, or a district. In effect, record keeping for a formatively based system can be made relatively easy for the classroom teacher with the help of proper technology.

Exercise 5.2 provides some review questions for this chapter. (See page 100 for a reproducible of this exercise and page 147 for a reproducible answer sheet. Visit **marzanoresearch.com/classroom strategiesthatwork** to download all the exercises and answers in this book.)

Exercise 5.2
Review Questions

The following questions address much of the important content in the chapter. Answer each one and then compare your answers with those on the corresponding answer sheet.

1. What are the defining characteristics of approach 1?
2. What are the defining characteristics of approach 2?
3. What are the defining characteristics of approach 3?
4. What are the defining characteristics of approach 4?
5. Which approach do you prefer and why?

Summary

This chapter discussed four different approaches to keeping track of student progress. Approaches 1, 2, and 4 address individual student progress, and approach 3 considers the progress of the class as a whole. Strengths and weaknesses of each approach were discussed, and examples of record keeping were provided. In all four approaches, students' current status and knowledge gain can be computed and celebrated. Although a paper/pencil approach can be used to track progress, technology provides tools that teachers can use to generate information specialized for individual students, for entire classrooms, and even for schools or districts.

Exercise 5.1

Record Keeping in the Four Approaches

The following questions address much of the content presented thus far. Answer each one and then compare your answers with those on the corresponding answer sheet.

1. While using approach 1, a particular student exhibits the following pattern of formative scores for a particular learning goal: 2.0, 2.5, 3.0, 3.5, and 2.5. Describe how you would determine the student's summative score. Make sure to explain your reasoning.

2. Explain why the 100-point scale can be used with approach 3 but not with approach 1 or 2.

3. Explain why it is not a good idea to automatically use the last score in a set of formative scores as the summative score, even if the final score comes from a final examination.

4. Explain why it is inappropriate to enter a score of 0 if a student misses an assessment or does not complete an assignment.

Exercise 5.2
Review Questions

The following questions address much of the important content in the chapter. Answer each one and then compare your answers with those provided on the corresponding answer sheet.

1. What are the defining characteristics of approach 1?

2. What are the defining characteristics of approach 2?

3. What are the defining characteristics of approach 3?

4. What are the defining characteristics of approach 4?

5. Which approach do you prefer and why?

Gradesheet for Approach 1

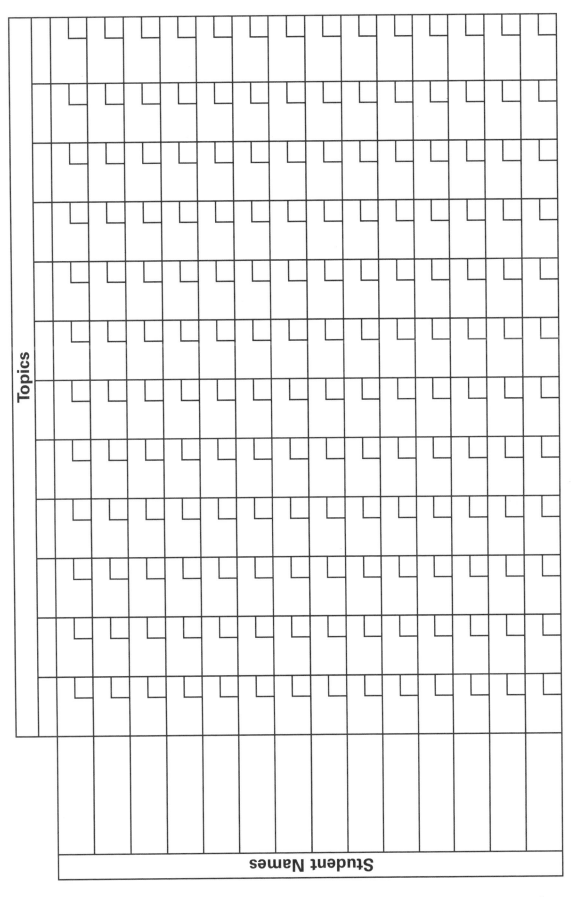

Topics

Student Names

Gradesheet for Approach 2

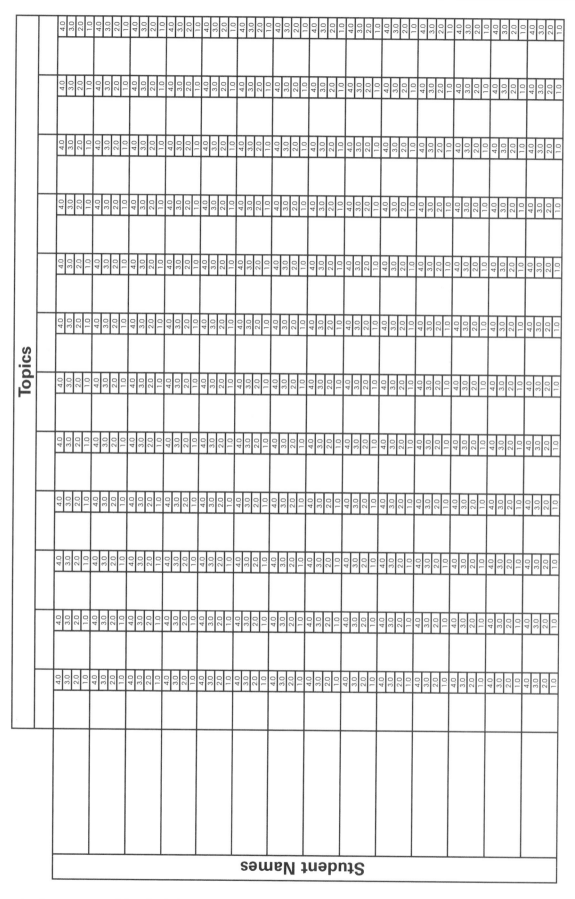

Topics

Student Names

Continual Progress Report

	0.0	0.5	1.0	1.5	2.0	2.5	3.0	3.5	4.0
Goal 1:									
Goal 2:									
Goal 3:									
Goal 4:									
Goal 5:									
Goal 6:									
Goal 7:									
Goal 8:									
Goal 9:									
Goal 10:									
Goal 11:									
Goal 12:									
Goal 13:									
Goal 14:									
Goal 15:									
Goal 16:									
Goal 17:									
Goal 18:									
Goal 19:									
Goal 20:									
Goal 21:									
Goal 22:									
Goal 23:									
Goal 24:									
Goal 25:									
Goal 26:									
Goal 27:									
Goal 28:									
Goal 29:									
Goal 30:									

Chapter 6

GRADING AND REPORTING

Ultimately, a teacher using the formative approach to assessment described in this book must address the issue of grades. In a later section of this chapter, we consider how a school or district might change its report card to accommodate a formatively based system. We begin, however, from the perspective of a teacher who must turn in an overall grade for each quarter, trimester, or semester in a school or district that utilizes traditional grades.

The Overall Grade

A teacher using any one of the four approaches described in chapter 5 can still translate student achievement into a traditional overall grade. Before addressing the issue of grading, though, it is necessary to revisit the issue of averaging. In chapter 2, a strong case was made that formative scores for a particular learning goal should not be averaged to construct a summative score. This, of course, is perfectly accurate, since averaging scores for a particular learning goal does not take into account that learning has occurred from one assessment to another. However, averaging is a viable option when performance *across* learning goals is being aggregated. For example, assume that a particular student has received the following summative scores for six learning goals addressed during the grading period: 2.5, 3.0, 2.0, 4.0, 3.0, and 3.5. The numeric average of 3.0 would be a good summary score representing typical final status for the student *across* the six learning goals.

Many districts and schools employ traditional A, B, C, D, and F letter grades. To translate the average score on the six learning goals into a grade, a simple guide is needed:

A = 3.00 to 4.00

B = 2.50 to 2.99

C = 2.00 to 2.49

D = 1.00 to 1.99

F = Below 1.00

In this system, the average score of 3.0 would be translated into a letter grade of A. The preceding example uses what is referred to as an "unweighted average." This simply means that all learning goals are considered equal—no goal has more weight than any other goal. Another approach is referred to as the "weighted average" approach. In this approach, some learning goals receive more weight in computing the average across goals (for a detailed discussion of weighted versus unweighted averages, see Marzano, 2006).

It is important to remember when considering overall letter grades (commonly referred to as a type of "omnibus grade") that any attempt to summarize a student's status across a variety of topics involves arbitrary decisions regarding where to end one grade designation and where to begin another. In the preceding example, the grade of A begins with an average of 3.0 for summative scores on learning goals. The grade of B ranges from 2.50 to 2.99, the grade of C from 2.00 to 2.49, and so on. There is a logic to this system. Namely, the A begins at 3.0 because a score of 3.0 indicates that a student has demonstrated understanding of all content in a target learning goal with no major errors or omissions. This makes some intuitive sense—if a student's average score indicates that he or she knows everything that was taught for the target learning goals, he or she should receive an A. The B range, 2.50 to 2.99, also has an intuitive logic to it. Having an average score within this range implies that across the learning goals that were addressed in a given grading period, the student typically demonstrated mastery of all of the basic content (score 2.0 content) and high partial mastery of the score 3.0 content that was directly taught for the target learning goals.

Some schools and districts like to use more refined categories such as A+, A, A–, and so on. The ranges for these grades are depicted in table 6.1.

Table 6.1 Conversion Scale to Traditional Grade

Average Scale Score Across Multiple Goals	Traditional Grade
3.75–4.00	A+
3.26–3.74	A
3.00–3.25	A–
2.84–2.99	B+
2.67–2.83	B
2.50–2.66	B–
2.34–2.49	C+
2.17–2.33	C
2.00–2.16	C–
1.76–1.99	D+
1.26–1.75	D
1.00–1.25	D–
Below 1.00	F

Translating summative scores for a grading period into an omnibus letter grade works fairly well for the first three approaches described in chapter 5. The fourth approach (the continual-improvement approach) provides a different perspective. As described in chapter 5, students in this system can continually raise their scores on learning goals that have previously been addressed. At any point in time, each student will have a tentative summative score on every learning goal that has been addressed thus far. The overall grade then involves all of the current tentative summative scores *up to that point in time*. To illustrate, consider a scenario in which ten learning goals were addressed in the first quarter and a specific student received the following scores:

Goal 1: 2.0

Goal 2: 2.5

Goal 3: 3.0

Goal 4: 2.0

Goal 5: 3.0

Goal 6: 2.5

Goal 7: 1.5

Goal 8: 2.0

Goal 9: 2.0

Goal 10: 3.0

The unweighted average for these ten scores is 2.35, which translates to a grade of C+.

The next quarter, ten more learning goals are addressed. The student receives the following scores on these ten goals:

Goal 11: 2.5

Goal 12: 2.0

Goal 13: 2.0

Goal 14: 3.0

Goal 15: 2.5

Goal 16: 3.0

Goal 17: 2.0

Goal 18: 1.5

Goal 19: 3.0

Goal 20: 2.0

However, during the second quarter, the student has raised his or her first-quarter scores as follows:

Goal 1: Increased from 2.0 to 3.0

Goal 2: Increased from 2.5 to 3.0

Goal 3: Stayed the same at 3.0

Goal 4: Increased from 2.0 to 3.0

Goal 5: Increased from 3.0 to 4.0

Goal 6: Increased from 2.5 to 3.0

Goal 7: Increased from 1.5 to 2.0

Goal 8: Increased from 2.0 to 3.0

Goal 9: Increased from 2.0 to 2.5

Goal 10: Stayed the same at 3.0

The second-quarter omnibus letter grade is based on the tentative summative scores for all twenty learning goals (ten most current scores from the first quarter and ten scores from the second quarter). The average score for these twenty goals is 2.65, which translates to a grade of B–.

This pattern would continue throughout the year. Consequently, the grade at the end of the year would be based on the current summative scores for all learning goals that have been addressed for the entire year.

The Conjunctive Approach

The approach discussed thus far relies on some type of averaging of scores on learning goals (weighted or unweighted). In general, schemes that are based on averaging are referred to as "compensatory approaches" in that a high score on one learning goal can compensate for a low score on another. For example, if a student receives a score of 1.0 on a particular learning goal, this can be offset by a score of 4.0 on another goal. The average of the two scores is 2.5.

In a conjunctive approach, minimum scores are established on each learning goal for specific grades. To illustrate, assume that nine learning goals were addressed in the first quarter of a given year. For each of these goals, a scale was developed as described in chapter 3. However, for goals 1, 2, and 5, the teacher did not progress past score 2.0 content in his or her lessons. Additionally, for goals 8 and 9, the teacher only began addressing score 3.0 content immediately before the end of the grading period. Given that for three of the learning goals, the class did not receive instruction beyond score 2.0, and for two other goals, the teacher provided partial instruction only on the score 3.0 content, the teacher might establish the following criteria for a grade of A:

Goal 1: 2.0 or above

Goal 2: 2.0 or above

Goal 3: 3.0 or above

Goal 4: 3.0 or above

Goal 5: 2.0 or above

Goal 6: 3.0 or above

Goal 7: 3.0 or above

Goal 8: 2.5 or above

Goal 9: 2.5 or above

Notice that in this scheme, a student can receive a grade of A with a score of 2.0 on goals 1, 2, and 5, and a score of 2.5 on goals 8 and 9.

For a grade of B, the teacher might establish the following minimum scores:

Goal 1: 1.5 or above

Goal 2: 1.5 or above

Goal 3: 2.5 or above

Goal 4: 2.5 or above

Goal 5: 1.5 or above

Goal 6: 2.5 or above

Goal 7: 2.5 or above

Goal 8: 2.0 or above

Goal 9: 2.0 or above

Similar minimum scores would be established for grades of C, D, and F. As this example illustrates, the conjunctive approach is very useful when a teacher has not addressed all levels of the scale for one or more learning goals during a grading period.

Translation to Advanced, Proficient, Basic, and Below Basic

A very popular alternative to an overall letter grade is a scale that uses the descriptors *advanced*, *proficient*, *basic*, and *below basic*. As described in chapter 1, this approach became popular in 1990 when the National Assessment of Educational Progress began using very similar categories. A translation to the scale is achieved fairly easily. To illustrate, consider table 6.2.

Table 6.2 Translation Scale for Descriptors

Advanced	Score 4.0	More complex learning goal
	Score 3.5	In addition to score 3.0 performance, partial success at score 4.0 content
Proficient	Score 3.0	Target learning goal
	Score 2.5	No major errors or omissions regarding score 2.0 content, and partial success at score 3.0 content
Basic	Score 2.0	Simpler learning goal
	Score 1.5	Partial success at score 2.0 content, but major errors or omissions regarding score 3.0 content
Below Basic	Score 1.0	With help, partial success at score 2.0 content and score 3.0 content
	Score 0.5	With help, partial success at score 2.0 content, but not at score 3.0 content
	Score 0.0	Even with help, no success

The logic of table 6.2 is fairly transparent. As explained in the book *Classroom Assessment and Grading That Work*,

> *Advanced* performance means that a student can go beyond what was presented in class, indicated by the score values of 4.0 and 3.5. *Proficient* performance means that a student exhibits no errors relative to the simple and complex ideas and processes, or the student exhibits no errors regarding the simpler details and processes and partial knowledge of more complex ideas and processes, indicated by the score values of 3.0 and 2.5, and so on. (Marzano, 2006, p. 57)

Although the logic of table 6.2 is straightforward, it is useful to keep in mind that "cut points" for each performance level are not absolute. The scale can be changed from one learning goal to the next, depending on the extent to which it has been addressed in class. If the teacher has not addressed score 3.0 content, for example, by the end of the grading period, the cut scores for proficient and advanced might be changed.

The Percentage Approach

Finally, some districts and schools require an overall percentage score at the end of each grading period. To arrive at a percentage score, the conversion scale in table 6.3 or an adaptation of it might be used.

Table 6.3 Conversion Scale to Percents

Scale Score	Percentage Score
4.0	100
3.5	95
3.0	90
2.5	80
2.0	70
1.5	65
1.0	60
Below 1.0	50

Teachers first translate scores on the scale to percentage scores and then average those percentages. To illustrate, reconsider the previous example of scale scores on six learning goals:

Goal 1 = 2.5 = 80%

Goal 2 = 3.0 = 90%

Goal 3 = 2.0 = 70%

Goal 4 = 4.0 = 100%

Goal 5 = 3.0 = 90%

Goal 6 = 3.5 = 95%

Average = 87.5%

Here the score of 2.5 on learning goal 1 translates to 80%, the score of 3.0 on learning goal 2 translates to 90%, and so on. The average of these percentage scores is 87.5%.

Exercise 6.1 provides some practice in converting scores. (See page 124 for a reproducible of this exercise and page 148 for a reproducible answer sheet. Visit **marzanoresearch.com/classroomstrat egiesthatwork** to download all the exercises and answers in this book.)

Exercise 6.1
Converting Scores

The following questions address much of the important content addressed thus far. Answer each one and then compare your answers with those provided on the corresponding answer sheet.

1. Explain why it is legitimate to compute an average across summative scores for different learning goals, but it is not legitimate to compute an average across formative scores within a given learning goal.

2. Assume that a student has attained the following summative scores on seven learning goals addressed during a grading period:

   Goal 1: 2.5

   Goal 2: 2.5

   Goal 3: 3.0

   Goal 4: 3.0

   Goal 5: 2.5

   Goal 6: 2.0

   Goal 7: 2.5

   A. Using the conversion scale in table 6.1 (page 106), compute the letter grade for the student.

   Average score: _____

   Average grade: _____

   B. Using the conversion scale in table 6.2 (page 109), translate the student's scores into one of the following categories: advanced, proficient, basic, or below basic.

   C. Using the conversion scale in table 6.3 (page 110), translate the student's scores into an average percentage score.

3. For the seven summative scores used in question 2, assume that during the grading period, the teacher has addressed only score 2.0 content for goals 6 and 7 and has just started score 3.0 content for goals 4 and 5. Devise a conjunctive approach that takes this into consideration, and compute a letter grade using the following matrix:

	Minimum Score for A	Minimum Score for B	Minimum Score for C	Minimum Score for D	Score for F
Goal 1					
Goal 2					
Goal 3					
Goal 4					
Goal 5					
Goal 6					
Goal 7					

Changing School and District Report Cards

Thus far, the discussion has been geared to the individual classroom teacher who wishes to provide students with formative feedback on specific learning goals even though he or she works in a traditional school that requires an omnibus grade of some form for each student. This section briefly describes how schools and entire districts can change to reflect student progress and status on specific learning goals. This, of course, is the ideal situation—an entire school system devoted to a formative reporting approach. For a more detailed discussion of the approaches described here, see Marzano (2006) and

Marzano and Haystead (2008). Here we consider two basic approaches to school and district report cards: a standards-referenced approach and a standards-based approach.

The distinction between a standards-referenced and a standards-based system was introduced in chapter 1. In a standards-referenced system, a student's achievement is reported (or referenced) in relationship to his or her position on the scales for specific learning goals. However, even if the student does not achieve a specific score on the scales for those goals, the student still moves on to new learning goals the next year when he or she has matriculated to a new grade level. In a standards-based system, students do not move on to a new level of content until they have mastered the content at their current level. We begin with a discussion of a standards-referenced approach.

A Standards-Referenced Approach

To design a standards-referenced system, a district must first reorganize or "reconstitute" state standards into a format that can be used to track student progress using formative and summative scores as described in chapters 2 through 5 of this text. The process starts by rewriting the standards at each grade level into a series of learning goals. Each goal is accompanied by a scale that has been constructed using the guidelines provided in chapters 3 through 5. In effect, the school or district creates the scales for all teachers at each grade level.

The learning goals are then organized into what we have referred to as measurement topics or reporting topics (see Marzano, 2006; Marzano & Haystead, 2008). For example, as described in *Designing and Teaching Learning Goals and Objectives* (Marzano, 2009), thirty-one learning goals might be identified in science for a particular grade level. These thirty-one goals would then be organized into eleven measurement topics, and these measurement topics might be organized into four strands. To illustrate, consider a topic titled Atmospheric Processes and the Water Cycle. It might contain the following two learning goals:

> *Goal 1*: Students will illustrate how climate patterns are affected by the water cycle and its processes.
>
> *Goal 2*: Students will model how all levels of the earth's atmosphere (troposphere, stratosphere, mesosphere, and thermosphere) are affected by temperature and pressure.

Additionally, that measurement topic might be housed within a strand referred to as Earth and Space Sciences along with two other measurement topics: Composition and Structure of the Earth, and Composition and Structure of the Universe.

Table 6.4 depicts K–8 measurement topics in mathematics that a district might design using state standards. Notice that there are twelve measurement topics organized into six large strands.

At the high school level, measurement topics with accompanying learning goals and scales would be designed for specific courses. For example, the following are sample measurement topics for three courses: Algebra I, Geometry, and Algebra II:

Algebra I

Formulas

Polynomial operations

Table 6.4 Measurement Topics for Mathematics

Mathematics	
Numbers and Operations	**Geometry**
1. Number sense and number systems	7. Lines, angles, and geometric objects
2. Operations and estimation	8. Transformation, congruency, and similarity
Computation	**Measurement**
3. Addition and subtraction	9. Measurement systems
4. Multiplication and division	10. Perimeter, area, and volume
Algebra and Functions	**Data Analysis and Probability**
5. Patterns, relations, and functions	11. Data organization and interpretation
6. Algebraic representations and mathematical models	12. Probability

Solving equations and inequalities in one variable

Radicals and factoring

Solving quadratic equations

Solving systems of linear equations

Rational expressions

Ratios, proportions, and percents

Graphing linear equations and inequalities

Word problems involving algebraic equations

Geometry

Applying the concept of deductive reasoning and proof

Applying the properties of points, segments, angles, lines, and their relationships

Polygon congruence and similarity

Triangle calculations: Pythagorean theorem and right triangle trigonometry

Polygon and circle measures

Perimeter, area, surface area, and volume

Transformational geometry

Probability

Algebra II

Radicals and exponent operations

Function operations

Systems of equations and matrices

Equation solving

Complex number operations

Modeling with equations/data analysis

Conic sections

Function graphing and transformations

Logarithmic and exponential equations

Using the scales designed by the district, each teacher provides summative scores on the learning goals for each student at the end of each grading period using one of the approaches described in chapter 5. These summative scores are then combined to obtain a score for a measurement topic. For example, assume a particular student received scores of 2.0 and 3.0 on the two learning goals that constitute a specific measurement topic. The summative score for the overall measurement topic would be considered the average of the two—2.5. Of course, an unweighted average is one of a number of ways that summative scores on learning goals can be combined to obtain a summative score for a measurement topic. As we have seen, weighted averages and conjunctive approaches (among others) can also be used.

For ease of communication to parents, some schools and districts like to compute scores for measurement topics that contain multiple learning goals using the same scale that is used for individual learning goals. For example, if the 0–4-point scale with half-point scores is used for learning goals, the same scale is used for measurement topics. This requires decisions about how to combine summative scores on learning goals within a measurement topic. For example, assume a particular measurement topic involves three learning goals and a particular student attains summative scores of 3.0, 3.0, and 2.0 on those three learning goals at the end of the grading period. The unweighted numeric average of those three summative scores is 2.67, but the school or district has determined that in the report card scores will be reported for each measurement topic using a scale that involves whole-point and half-point scores only. Thus, the 2.67 must be converted to a whole-point or half-point score. Simply rounding the score of 2.67 to a 3.0 addresses this issue. Of course, if the district or school does not combine learning goals into measurement topics but instead reports the summative scores on each learning goal, then the issue is averted. However, the report card will contain quite a few learning goals for each subject area. Figure 6.1 depicts a report card that uses measurement topics and a scale that involves whole-point and half-point scores for those measurement topics.

The sample report card in figure 6.1 is for fourth grade, but it easily generalizes down to kindergarten and up to grade 12. The primary difference at the high school level would be that courses as opposed to subject areas would be the focus of the report card.

For discussion purposes, we will assume that the school using this report card is departmentalized at the fourth-grade level—different teachers are responsible for each subject area as opposed to a single teacher being responsible for all subject areas as in the case of a self-contained classroom.

Summative scores on measurement topics are reported as bar graphs within each subject area. The student in figure 6.1 has a summative score of 2.5 for the measurement topic of Word Recognition and Vocabulary in language arts; he has a summative score of 3.0 for the topic of Estimation in mathematics, and so on. Note that the left-hand part of each bar is darker than the right-hand part of each bar. The darker part represents a student's status at the beginning of the grading period. Thus, the lighter part represents the student's knowledge gain during the grading period.

Name:	John Mark
Address:	123 Some Street
City:	Anytown, CO 80000
Grade Level:	4
Homeroom:	Ms. Smith

Subject	Score	Grade		Skill	Score	Grade
Language Arts	2.46	C		Participation	3.40	A
Mathematics	2.50	B		Work Completion	2.90	B
Science	2.20	C		Behavior	3.40	A
Social Studies	3.10	A		Working in Groups	2.70	B
Art	3.00	A				

	Score	0.5	1.0	1.5	2.0	2.5	3.0	3.5	4.0
Language Arts									
Reading:									
Word Recognition and Vocabulary	2.5								
Reading for Main Idea	1.5								
Literary Analysis	2.0								
Writing:									
Language Conventions	3.5								
Organization and Focus	2.5								
Research and Technology	1.0								
Evaluation and Revision	2.5								
Writing Applications	3.0								
Listening and Speaking:									
Comprehension	3.0								
Organization and Delivery	3.0								
Analysis and Evaluation of Oral Media	2.5								
Speaking Applications	2.5								
Life Skills:									
Participation	4.0								
Work Completion	3.5								
Behavior	3.5								
Working in Groups	3.0								
Average for Language Arts	2.46								
Mathematics									
Number Systems	3.5								
Estimation	3.0								

Figure 6.1 Sample report card depicting a standards-referenced approach.

Continued on next page →

Addition/Subtraction	2.5
Multiplication/Division	2.5
Ratio/Proportion/Percent	1.0
Life Skills:	
Participation	4.0
Work Completion	2.0
Behavior	3.5
Working in Groups	2.0
Average for Mathematics	2.50
Science	
Matter and Energy	2.0
Forces of Nature	2.5
Diversity of Life	1.5
Human Identity	3.5
Interdependence of Life	1.5
Life Skills:	
Participation	3.0
Work Completion	1.5
Behavior	2.5
Working in Groups	1.0
Average for Science	2.20
Social Studies	
The Influence of Culture	3.5
Current Events	3.0
Personal Responsibility	4.0
Government Representation	3.5
Human and Civil Rights	1.5
Life Skills:	
Participation	3.5
Work Completion	3.5
Behavior	3.5
Working in Groups	4.0

Average for Social Studies	3.10									
Art										
Purposes of Art	3.5									
Art Skills	3.0									
Art and Culture	2.5									
Life Skills:										
Participation	2.5									
Work Completion	4.0									
Behavior	4.0									
Working in Groups	3.5									
Average for Art	3.00									

Notice that the report card in figure 6.1 contains measurement topics for life skills. Specifically, each subject area reports scores for the following life skills: participation, work completion, behavior, and working in groups. Although we have not addressed scales for these types of skills, they are easily constructed using the generic scale presented in chapter 3. To illustrate, consider table 6.5 (page 118).

In table 6.5, specific behaviors have been identified that illustrate score 2.0, 3.0, and 4.0 competence for the life skill of work completion at grades 6 through 8. For a listing of other scales for life skills, see Marzano and Haystead (2008).

At the top of the report card in figure 6.1 are traditional omnibus letter grades; these were generated using the schemes described in the first part of this chapter. Summative score (and knowledge gain) bar graphs are reported for each student in the life skills in each subject area. However, the omnibus grade for each subject area does not include these life-skills scores. Specifically, figure 6.1 shows that in language arts, the student received summative scores of 4.0, 3.5, 3.5, and 3.0 for the life skills of participation, work completion, behavior, and working in groups, respectively. These life-skills scores were not included when computing the average scale score of 2.46 for language arts (the average for language arts is reported next to the letter grade for language arts). That average for language arts is based solely on the measurement topics that deal with language arts content. To compute the life-skills grades listed at the top right of the report card, the life-skills scores were averaged across subject areas. For example, the student's average score of 3.40 for the life skill of participation (see the top right section of figure 6.1) was computed using the student's participation scores across the subject areas.

A report card like that in figure 6.1 could be accompanied by a traditional transcript that lists courses taken, credits earned (in the case of high school), and an overall grade point average (GPA). As mentioned previously, this report card (and variations of it) is referred to as "standards-referenced." In a standards-referenced system, students do not have to demonstrate proficiency in each measurement topic to move on to another grade level. Requiring students to demonstrate competence in all content is the domain of a standards-based system.

Table 6.5 Scale for Work Completion

Work Completion	
Middle School (Grades 6–8)	
Score 4.0	The student is successful with the more complex details and behaviors such as: • Developing and implementing complex time-management plans for assignments (for example, creating a project organizer to track progress on a long-term assignment such as a research paper) No major errors or omissions regarding the score 4.0 content
Score 3.5	In addition to score 3.0 performance, partial success at score 4.0 content
Score 3.0	The student meets all required expectations regarding work completion such as: • Handing in assignments that meet format requirements specified by the teacher (for example, proper heading, margins, and citations) • Developing and implementing basic time-management plans for assignments (for example, creating a homework organizer to track due dates for various assignments) • Completing assignments on time and providing acceptable explanations when assignments are not handed in on time (for example, having a plausible explanation that meets established classroom policy regarding late assignments) No major errors or omissions regarding the score 3.0 content
Score 2.5	No major errors or omissions regarding the score 2.0 content, and partial success at score 3.0 content
Score 2.0	The student is successful with the simpler details and behaviors such as: • Recognizing or recalling accurate statements about the format requirements for a given assignment • Recognizing or recalling accurate statements about the elements of basic time-management plans (for example, identifying a basic homework organizer and recognizing due dates, descriptions, and specific tasks as things that should be included for each assignment) • Recognizing or recalling deadlines for assignments (for example, using a simple chart to keep track of the due date for each assignment) No major errors or omissions regarding the score 2.0 content
Score 1.5	Partial success at score 2.0 content, but major errors or omissions regarding score 3.0 content
Score 1.0	With help, partial success at score 2.0 content and score 3.0 content
Score 0.5	With help, partial success at score 2.0 content, but not at score 3.0 content
Score 0.0	Even with help, no success

Exercise 6.2 provides some practice in standards-referenced reporting. (See page 126 for a reproducible of this exercise and page 150 for a reproducible answer sheet. Visit **marzanoresearch.com/ classroomstrategiesthatwork** to download all the exercises and answers in this book.)

Exercise 6.2
Standards-Referenced Reporting

The following questions address much of the important content addressed thus far. Use figure 6.1 (page 115) to answer each question, and then compare your answers with those provided on the corresponding answer sheet.

1. Show how the student received an average score of 2.70 for working in groups.
2. Show how the student received an average score of 3.10 for social studies.
3. Identify the topic or topics for which the student exhibited the most gain over the grading period.
4. Identify the topic or topics for which the student showed the least gain over the grading period.

A Standards-Based Approach

In a standards-based system, students are not locked into a specific grade level based on their age. Rather, for each subject area, they move up and down a continuum of knowledge or skill based on their demonstrated competence. Thus, in a pure standards-based approach, there are no grade levels per se. There are simply "levels" of knowledge and skill for each subject area. Table 6.6 depicts an individual student's status across various subject areas in a pure standards-based system.

Table 6.6 A Standards-Based Report Card

Level	Art	Career Literacy	Math	Personal/ Social Skills	Language Arts	Science	Social Studies	Technology
(Advanced) 3								
(Advanced) 2								
(Advanced) 1								
10								
09								
08								
07								
06								
05								
04		2 of 16	21 of 35		3 of 36	17 of 25		
03	9 of 10	3.0 (Proficient)	3.0 (Proficient)	4 of 6	4.0 (Advanced)	3.0 (Proficient)	13 of 15	7 of 8
02	3.0 (Proficient)	3.0 (Proficient)	4.0 (Advanced)	3.0 (Proficient)	3.0 (Proficient)	3.0 (Proficient)	3.0 (Proficient)	4.0 (Advanced)
01	3.0 (Proficient)	3.0 (Proficient)	4.0 (Advanced)	3.0 (Proficient)	3.0 (Proficient)	3.0 (Proficient)	3.0 (Proficient)	3.0 (Proficient)

Note: Shaded cells indicate levels that do not apply to the subject area.

Notice that in table 6.6, most subject areas include levels 1 to 10. Level 10 represents mastery of the content expected for a general high school diploma. Not all subject areas have ten levels, however. Art has six levels, technology has seven levels, and personal/social skills has five levels. This convention is used because in a standards-based system, content is not organized into grade levels that are based on age. It is instead organized into levels based on the nature of the content. While the content necessary for high school graduation might logically fall into ten levels for some subjects, it might fall into fewer levels for others. This convention is in line with the current movement toward developing learning progressions as described in chapter 1—organizing content into natural progressions of information and skill as opposed to artificial levels based on age (grade levels). Also, note that each subject area in table 6.6 has one or more advanced levels students might attain. These levels are for students who wish to further their learning beyond what is required for high school graduation.

In a standards-based system, students receive instruction in each subject area at their appropriate levels. This is accomplished by having students move to different teachers for each subject. For example, the student in table 6.6 would meet with the level 4 mathematics teacher for mathematics, the level 3 teacher for social studies, and so on. Of course, this generates rather large logistics, scheduling, and staffing issues. Another option is to have teachers teach to multiple levels. For example, a given mathematics teacher might address levels 1 through 3. During his or her mathematics class, he or she would work with students at each of these levels. Another mathematics teacher would work with students in levels 4 through 6, and so on. For an excellent discussion of how such systems might be developed and organized, see DeLorenzo, Battino, Schreiber, and Gaddy-Carrio (2009).

The final feature to take note of in the report card in table 6.6 is how a student's current status is reported. Consider the student's status in mathematics. In that subject, he or she is working on level 4. Note that this level has a ratio of 21/35 recorded. This means that the student has demonstrated score 3.0 or higher competence on twenty-one of the thirty-five learning goals at that level. He or she must demonstrate score 3.0 or higher competence on fourteen more learning goals to progress to level 5 in mathematics. In language arts, the student has a ratio of 3/36 and must demonstrate score 3.0 or higher competence in thirty-three more learning goals to move to the next level.

Because no overall grades are computed in standards-based systems and because of the emphasis on demonstrating proficiency in each and every learning goal before a student progresses to the next level, reporting is typically focused on learning goals as opposed to measurement topics. This is why each ratio recorded in table 6.6 reports the number of learning goals for which score 3.0 proficiency or higher has been attained and the number of learning goals still remaining.

For some schools and districts, getting rid of traditional grade levels represents too radical a shift from the norm. Stated differently, some schools and districts desire to employ a standards-based approach but maintain traditional grade levels. Fortunately, there is a way to do this. The most straightforward approach to implementing a standards-based system while maintaining traditional grade levels is to treat grade levels as performance levels. The record-keeping system up to grade 8 is depicted in table 6.7.

Notice that table 6.7 is basically identical to table 6.6 except that it lists grade levels. Each grade level represents a level of knowledge or skill defined by specific learning goals for which specific scales have been developed.

Table 6.8 depicts a report card at the high school level. At this level, specific courses are listed for each subject area from simple to complex. For example, in mathematics, Algebra I addresses simpler content than Algebra II, and so on. It is important to note that at the high school level, some courses might not exhibit a strict hierarchic structure. For example, it might be the case that in technology, Desktop Publishing does not have to be taken before Digital Graphics and Animation. In any course, once the student has demonstrated mastery (score 3.0 content) for all of the learning goals within a course, he or she will receive credit for that course.

Table 6.7 Standards-Based Reporting for Grades K–8

Grade	Art	Career Literacy	Math	Personal/ Social Skills	Language Arts	Science	Social Studies	Technology
8								
7								
6								
5			4 of 32					
4		7 of 11	3.0 (Proficient)		7 of 31	2 of 23		
3		3.0 (Proficient)	4.0 (Advanced)	2 of 6	3.0 (Proficient)	4.0 (Advanced)		
2	9 of 10	3.0 (Proficient)	3.0 (Proficient)	3.0 (Proficient)	4.0 (Advanced)	3.0 (Proficient)	2 of 15	7 of 8
1	3.0 (Proficient)	3.0 (Proficient)	4.0 (Advanced)	3.0 (Proficient)	3.0 (Proficient)	3.0 (Proficient)	3.0 (Proficient)	4.0 (Advanced)
K	3.0 (Proficient)	3.0 (Proficient)	4.0 (Advanced)	3.0 (Proficient)	3.0 (Proficient)	3.0 (Proficient)	3.0 (Proficient)	3.0 (Proficient)

Table 6.8 Standards-Based Reporting for High School

Subject Area	Course	Score
Mathematics	Calculus	
	Geometry	
	Algebra II	12 of 24
	Algebra I	3.0 (proficient)
Science	AP Environmental Science	
	Physics	
	Chemistry	6 of 22
	Biology	3.0 (proficient)
Social Studies	Economics	
	World History	11 of 21
	U.S. History	4.0 (advanced)
	Geography	3.0 (proficient)
Language Arts	Shakespeare	
	Ancient Literature	13 of 22
	European Literature	3.0 (proficient)
	U.S. Literature	3.0 (proficient)
Art	Orchestra	
	Performing Arts	9 of 21
	Painting	3.0 (proficient)
Technology	Digital Graphics and Animation	
	Desktop Publishing	17 of 22
	Computer Science	4.0 (advanced)

As in the case with the standards-based system that does not use grade levels, an overall omnibus grade is not assigned to students when grade levels are used as performance levels. Rather, the "report card" depicted in tables 6.7 and 6.8 is kept current at all times. Again, a ratio is recorded at each grade level in which the student is working for each subject area. This ratio represents the number of learning goals for which the student has demonstrated score 3.0 or higher competence.

Examining the patterns in tables 6.6, 6.7, and 6.8, it is evident that the lowest score a student can receive in any learning goal at any level, grade level, or course is a 3.0. This is because students must demonstrate a score of 3.0 on each learning goal to move on to the next level, grade level, or course. However, there can still be discriminations made between students as to their performances within each level, grade level, or course. To illustrate, consider table 6.7. Notice that at grade 1, the student achieved a score of advanced in mathematics and technology and a score of proficient in all other subjects. Recall that at each grade level, students are scored on a 0–4-point scale for each learning goal. If a student has achieved a 4.0 on all (or the majority) of the learning goals for a given subject at a given grade level, he or she can be awarded the status of advanced as opposed to proficient.

As is the case with the approach to standards-based schooling that does not use grade levels, scheduling is an issue with the grade-level standards-based approach. One way to address scheduling is to organize schools into grade-level bands. This is depicted in table 6.9.

Table 6.9 Grade-Level Bands

High School (9–12)
Remedial
Advanced
6–8
Remedial
Advanced
3–5
Remedial
Advanced
K–2
Remedial

Table 6.9 depicts four grade-level bands: K–2, 3–5, 6–8, and 9–12. Within a grade-level band, classes are offered for core subject areas at the same time. For example, within the 3–5 grade-level band, all mathematics is offered at the same time, all science is offered at the same time, and so on. Additionally, within a grade-level band, instructional opportunities have to be provided for the students working above the interval and below the interval. For example, when mathematics is being offered in the 3–5 grade-level band, instruction is also provided for students who are working above the fifth-grade level. This is depicted in the row titled "advanced" in the 3–5 grade-level band in table 6.9. The emphasis with these students is to allow them to progress as rapidly as they wish through the mathematics content from grade 6 and beyond. Likewise, instruction must be provided for students who are working below the third grade when mathematics is being offered. This is depicted in the row titled "remedial" in the 3–5 grade-level band in table 6.9. The emphasis with these students is to bring them up to the third-grade level (at least) as quickly as possible.

An advantage the grade-level approach to standards-based schooling has over the approach that does not use grade levels is that it allows students to stay with their cohort groups—their grade-level peers. For example, in each grade, students could still have a homeroom period and activities that are specific to that grade level. High school would still maintain freshman, sophomore, junior, and senior classes. This concept of grade-level cohorts appears to be deeply engrained in U.S. society and does not have to be discarded to implement a standards-based system. However, at any point in time, students are working on the content appropriate to their current level of understanding and skill.

While there are many details a district must work out to implement a standards-based system that uses grade levels or a standards-based system that does not use grade levels, the effort would appear to be balanced by the potential benefits of students being able to move through content at a pace that optimizes their learning.

Exercise 6.3 provides some practice in standards-based reporting. (See page 127 for a reproducible of this exercise and page 152 for a reproducible answer sheet. Visit **marzanoresearch.com/classroomstrategiesthatwork** to download all the exercises and answers in this book.)

Exercise 6.3
Standards-Based Reporting

The following questions deal with much of the important content in this chapter. Answer each one and then compare your answers with those provided on the corresponding answer sheet.

1. In table 6.6 (page 119), explain what "3 of 36" for level 4 in language arts means.
2. In table 6.6, explain why art and technology have fewer levels than the other subject areas.
3. Explain why an overall grade cannot be assigned in a standards-based approach.
4. Explain how the "grade-level" standards-based approach differs from the standards-based approach that does not use grade levels.

Summary

This chapter discussed how teachers using any of the formative approaches discussed in previous chapters can address the issue of grades. Scale scores can be translated into omnibus grades, descriptors (advanced, proficient, basic, and below basic), and/or percentage scores. Consequently, teachers working in a traditional system can still take a formatively based approach in their assessments. Grading and grade reporting according to standards-referenced and standards-based approaches were also addressed. This level of change would require that an entire system make a commitment to a formatively based approach to standards-referenced or standards-based schooling.

Exercise 6.1

Converting Scores

The following questions address much of the important content addressed thus far. Answer each one and then compare your answers with those provided on the corresponding answer sheet.

1. Explain why it is legitimate to compute an average across summative scores for different learning goals, but it is not legitimate to compute an average across formative scores within a given learning goal.

2. Assume that a student has attained the following summative scores on seven learning goals addressed during a grading period:

   Goal 1: 2.5

   Goal 2: 2.5

   Goal 3: 3.0

   Goal 4: 3.0

   Goal 5: 2.5

   Goal 6: 2.0

   Goal 7: 2.5

   A. Using the conversion scale in table 6.1 (page 106), compute the letter grade for the student.

      Average score: _____

      Average grade: _____

   B. Using the conversion scale in table 6.2 (page 109), translate the student's scores into one of the following categories: advanced, proficient, basic, or below basic.

   C. Using the conversion scale in table 6.3 (page 110), translate the student's scores into an average percentage score.

3. For the seven summative scores used in question 2, assume that during the grading period, the teacher has addressed only score 2.0 content for goals 6 and 7 and has just started score 3.0 content for goals 4 and 5. Devise a conjunctive approach that takes this into consideration, and compute a letter grade using the following matrix:

	Minimum Score for A	Minimum Score for B	Minimum Score for C	Minimum Score for D	Score for F
Goal 1					
Goal 2					
Goal 3					
Goal 4					
Goal 5					
Goal 6					
Goal 7					

Exercise 6.2

Standards-Referenced Reporting

The following questions address much of the important content addressed thus far. Use figure 6.1 (pages 115–117) to answer each question, and then compare your answers with those provided on the corresponding answer sheet.

1. Show how the student received an average score of 2.70 for working in groups.

2. Show how the student received an average score of 3.10 for social studies.

3. Identify the topic or topics for which the student exhibited the most gain over the grading period.

4. Identify the topic or topics for which the student showed the least gain over the grading period.

Exercise 6.3

Standards-Based Reporting

The following questions deal with much of the important content in this chapter. Answer each one and then compare your answers with those provided on the corresponding answer sheet.

1. In table 6.6 (page 119), explain what "3 of 36" for level 4 in language arts means.

2. In table 6.6, explain why art and technology have fewer levels than the other subject areas.

3. Explain why an overall grade cannot be assigned in a standards-based approach.

4. Explain how the "grade-level" standards-based approach differs from the standards-based approach that does not use grade levels.

EPILOGUE

This book has been about radical change in the practice of classroom assessment and grading—two areas that are at the core of K–12 schooling in the United States. Classroom assessment must be executed in a formative manner if it is to be used as a tool to enhance student achievement. Grades must be based on a formative approach to classroom assessment so that they can reflect student status at the end of a grading period and not penalize students for initial misunderstandings or "slow starts" regarding specific topics. Ultimately, though, the entire K–12 system must change to allow students to progress at their own pace regarding subject-matter content.

While this book was written for individual classroom teachers working in traditional schools, it can be used to stimulate radical change at the school and district levels. Specifically, if individual teachers demonstrate the power of the techniques outlined in this book, other teachers will emulate their behavior. It will be a relatively small step for the administrators of an entire school or district to make a similar transformation once there is a critical mass of teachers who have transformed their classrooms.

APPENDIX A

ANSWERS TO EXERCISES

Answers to Exercise 2.1

Obtrusive, Unobtrusive, and Student-Generated Assessments

1. *Mona is very close to receiving an A on the content that has been covered in her art class this quarter. She approaches the teacher and proposes that she will provide a sketch that shows she has mastered the techniques presented during the quarter.*

    Mona is employing student-generated assessment in this scenario. She has designed an assessment that will demonstrate her mastery of the content.

2. *After teaching the concept of a thesis statement, discussing examples of successful thesis statements, and providing the students with opportunities for practice, Mr. Grace gives his students a topic and asks them to write a corresponding thesis statement. He scores the effectiveness of the thesis statements using a rubric and records the scores for each student.*

    Obtrusive assessment is being employed in this scenario. Mr. Grace has provided his students with instruction and practice, and he is now directly administering an assessment for which he will record a score for each student.

3. *After teaching a unit on editing and revising, Ms. Minturn asks her students to pull out a hard copy of an essay they composed earlier in the year. She breaks the class into pairs and asks them to read and suggest edits and revisions on their partners' essays. She collects the revisions and grades each student on the effectiveness of his or her editing.*

    Obtrusive assessment is being employed in this scenario. The teacher has provided a structured editing activity, and the work students are asked to do is graded and recorded by Ms. Minturn.

4. *Mr. Davis is teaching a unit on shading. He takes his class to an outside garden, and while the students are creating compositions focusing on the shadows and colors they see, he walks around and observes their progress. Without interrupting, he records an assessment score for each student in his gradebook.*

    Unobtrusive assessment is being employed in this scenario. Mr. Davis is assessing the work of his students, and he is recording their scores, but in a way that does not interrupt their work. It is possible that the students are not even aware of the assessment.

5. *Ms. Lewis has been working with her students on a cooperative learning goal. While she is monitoring recess, she notices four of them working together to complete a double-dutch jump rope game. Because all four students have to*

cooperate to reach their goal, Ms. Lewis decides these students have fulfilled the requirement for score 3.0 on the rubric she has designed for cooperative skills.

Unobtrusive assessment is being employed in this scenario. Ms. Lewis is observing her students, but they are unaware they are being assessed. She determines they have reached a score 3.0, and she records that score for each of the four students.

Answers to Exercise 2.2

Instructional Feedback Versus Formative Scores

1. *Ms. Levine is teaching a unit on oral communication. At the end of the unit, students will give an oral presentation on a book of their choosing, but Ms. Levine knows students need opportunities to practice skills such as eye contact, enunciation, and pace and volume control. To provide those opportunities, Ms. Levine asks the students more direct questions than she ordinarily might. The student who answers is asked to stand and address the class so that he or she may become a bit more comfortable with speaking in front of a group. Ms. Levine provides spontaneous feedback as well, such as suggesting that a student slow down or speak louder.*

   This scenario exemplifies the use of assessment as instructional feedback. Ms. Levine is not recording scores for her students. She is only providing opportunities for them to practice their public speaking as well as providing feedback to help them in the future.

2. *After a unit on the circulatory system, Mr. Williams asks students to complete a written test. He grades each one and records the scores.*

   This scenario exemplifies the use of assessment for formative scores. The written test is formal, and the grades are recorded.

3. *Ms. Bowman has given her students updates on their current scores for each learning goal covered during the first quarter of the school year. Candice has been reminded that her score for a goal involving immigration is a 2.5 on a 4-point rubric, and she wants to raise that score to a 3.0 by the end of the quarter. She approaches Ms. Bowman with an idea to create a family tree depicting the names of each family member on her mother's side, the countries from which they came, and the date of their arrival. Candice believes this would demonstrate her knowledge of the score 3.0 content.*

   This scenario exemplifies the use of assessment for formative scores. Candice is the one seeking to improve her grade and designing an assessment she believes will demonstrate she is deserving of a higher score, but the family tree is still an assessment, and the grade will be recorded.

4. *Mr. McKimm is teaching a unit on quadratic equations. He writes an equation and its solution on the blackboard and asks the class to vote on whether the solution is correct or incorrect. He chooses one student to explain why he or she thinks the solution is correct and one to explain why he or she thinks the solution is incorrect. After hearing both sides, the students vote again. Mr. McKimm makes a mental note of how many students appear to understand the problem.*

   This scenario exemplifies the use of assessment for instructional feedback. Mr. McKimm is not recording scores here; he is merely providing students with opportunities to think independently and learn from their mistakes.

1 of 2

5. *Ms. Walker is teaching a unit on volleyball. After covering individual skills with the students, she has split them up into teams. During one of the games, she notices that Ashley executes a perfect overhand serve. Ashley has had trouble with this skill, receiving low scores in the past. After seeing the serve, Ms. Walker makes a mental note to assign Ashley a higher score in the gradebook.*

This scenario exemplifies the use of assessment for formative scores. Although Ashley is not aware that she is being assessed, Ms. Walker has seen the level of execution she is looking for and will record Ashley's score.

Answers to Exercise 2.3
Review Questions

1. *What are the three types of classroom assessment, and what are some of the unique qualities of each?*

   The three types of classroom assessment are obtrusive assessment, unobtrusive assessment, and student-generated assessment. Obtrusive assessment is characterized by its formality. Classroom activity is suspended, and students "take a test." They know they are being assessed, and most often the assessment is scheduled and students are notified ahead of time. Unobtrusive assessment, by contrast, is characterized by its informality. Students most often are not aware they are being assessed. Instead, the teacher simply observes the students in action and gleans necessary information about their proficiencies. Student-generated assessment is characterized by the control it gives the student. As opposed to a teacher giving a formal or informal assessment, a student independently comes to a teacher with a specific idea of how he or she can demonstrate proficiency on a learning goal.

2. *What are the three ways to use assessments, and what are some of the unique characteristics of each?*

   The three uses of assessment are formative scores, summative scores, and instructional feedback. Formative scores are snapshots of a student's level of understanding or skill at a particular point in time, and they are recorded. Formative scores are meant to be used in conjunction with one another so that a teacher can get an overall picture of a student's achievement across an interval of time such as a grading period. Summative scores, by contrast, do not reflect a single performance on an assessment. Instead, they represent the teacher's overall judgment of a student's performance over a period of time. All of the formative scores lead up to the summative score. Instructional feedback is an assessment that may or may not be scored but is not recorded. It is meant to provide students with immediate information about their performance.

3. *What is the difference between formative assessment and formative scores as defined in* Formative Assessment and Standards-Based Grading*?*

   Formative assessment is a process, whereas a formative score refers to a specific assessment used in the process of formative assessment. Formative scores provide teachers with the data necessary to construct summative scores.

4. *Describe how assessments can provide information to teachers about their own performances.*

   Assessments can let teachers know what information needs to be reviewed or retaught. If a large group of students does not do well on a particular assessment, the teacher knows that that information needs to be revisited.

Answers to Exercise 3.1

Simpler and More Complex Content for Learning Goals

1. *Students will be able to multiply two-digit numbers by two-digit numbers.*

   Because the content in the target learning goal involves the expectation of a specific procedure, the more complex content will be a more difficult or more complex execution, and the simpler content will be a simpler execution. For example, more complex content might be multiplying three-digit numbers by two- or three-digit numbers, and simpler content might be multiplying one-digit numbers by one- or two-digit numbers.

2. *Students will be able to label the world's continents on a map.*

   The target goal here involves a specific level of geographic knowledge. The more complex content would likely be more detailed geographic knowledge, such as labeling all of the countries in North America and the larger countries on each of the other continents. The simpler content will likely require only basic geographic knowledge, such as labeling only the Americas on a map, or recognizing the names of the world's continents.

3. *Students will be able to sing with correct tempo and pitch.*

   The target goal specifies the process of singing with expectations of correct tempo and pitch. The more complex content would include more aspects of singing, such as singing with attention to tempo, pitch, key, and volume. It might also require students to sing with correct tempo and pitch in various situations such as singing in rounds. Finally, it could ask students to sing more difficult songs with correct tempo and pitch, or to hear when they are off and correct themselves. The simpler content might ask students to sing with correct tempo and pitch when accompanied by a group, or it could ask students to sing simpler songs with attention to tempo and pitch.

4. *Students will be able to discuss the major cause-and-effect relationships in a narrative story.*

   The more complex content for this goal could involve asking students to draw comparisons between the cause-and-effect relationships in two or more stories. It might also ask students to imagine what might have happened in the story if one or more events had not happened or had happened differently. The simpler content might simply require students to recognize accurate statements about the major cause-and-effect relationships in a narrative story. It might also ask students to recognize some vocabulary terms and phrases.

5. *Students will be able to discuss how the earth changes through both fast processes and slow processes.*

More complex content for this target goal could ask students to trace a specific slow process in an area near them or discuss in detail the changes that resulted from a specific natural disaster. It could also ask them to study one or more of the earth's processes and map where they are most likely to occur. Simpler content might ask students to list the earth's fast and slow processes or recognize accurate statements about them.

Formative Assessment and Standards-Based Grading • © 2010 Marzano Research Laboratory • marzanoresearch.com
Visit **marzanoresearch.com/classroomstrategiesthatwork** to download this page.

Answers to Exercise 3.2

Scoring Assessments Using the Scale

1. *Mr. Swanson has set up an activity that allows the students in his physical education class to demonstrate their ability to balance themselves. Some parts of the activity ask students to demonstrate the simpler aspects of the goal (score 2.0 content), such as approaching the balancing activity slowly and with a firm foundation. Other parts of the activity ask students to demonstrate target behaviors, such as walking on a balance beam (score 3.0 content), and some parts of the activity ask students to demonstrate behaviors above and beyond the target learning goal, such as throwing a ball to a partner while balancing or catching themselves when they begin to fall (score 4.0 content). Bonnie exhibits ability in the simpler balance activities and has some success at the target balance activities.*

   Since Bonnie has exhibited mastery of the simpler elements, she has achieved at least a score 2.0. Since she has not performed all of the elements designed for the target learning goal, she has not yet achieved a score 3.0. Because she did perform some of the elements, though, her score would be a 2.5.

2. *For a learning goal regarding speaking fluency, Mrs. Jass has assigned the students in her French class a brief oral report on the topic of food. Students must use some basic vocabulary words relevant to the topic (score 2.0 content). They must also use complete sentences to discuss how the meal habits of the French are different from the meal habits in the United States (score 3.0 content). Finally, Mrs. Jass asks them to offer a few sentences about which food culture (French or American) they prefer and why (score 4.0 content). Ida exhibits the ability to pronounce the relevant vocabulary words provided and the ability to speak in simple sentences about the topic clearly and fluently. Though she does not have a strong opinion on the topic, she clearly expresses the advantages of each culture.*

   Because Ida demonstrated fluency with the required vocabulary words, her score is at least a 2.0. Additionally, she has clearly put together the sentences the score 3.0 content asks for. Finally, she has demonstrated the fluency required for score 4.0. She did not have a strong opinion, but since the goal focuses on fluency, this does not factor into the score.

3. *Mr. Gage has assigned a short language arts paper that will allow him to assess the students on a learning goal regarding the use of research in a persuasive composition. In the directions, he has provided a topic and asked the students to take one of two possible positions. In order to persuade the audience, he has asked them to find two valid research sources (score 2.0 content). He has also asked them to use direct quotations from those sources to support their chosen positions (score 3.0 content). Finally, he has asked that they address any possible*

counterclaims they see as relevant (score 4.0 content). Caroline's assignment demonstrates that she has found two valid sources of support for her chosen position; however, while the composition mentions both of those sources, it does not directly quote either, and no counterclaim is addressed.

Caroline has clearly not demonstrated proficiency at the score 4.0 content, and while she mentions the sources in the paper, a score of 3.0 requires direct quotations, so she has not demonstrated even partial score 3.0 proficiency either. She did, however, find two valid research resources, which indicates a score of 2.0.

4. *Ms. Satrom has noticed that Jasper did not do well on a particular mathematics test. The test asked the students to read a word problem and translate it into a mathematical equation (score 2.0 content), solve the equation (score 3.0 content), and compare the final answer to the original word problem to see if the answer makes sense (score 4.0 content). She calls Jasper in for an individual meeting and goes through one of the problems with him. While he was not able to solve the problem on his own, he is able to create a mathematical equation and solve it with some guidance and prompting from Ms. Satrom.*

Because Jasper was not able to demonstrate mastery of any of the content on his own, his score is below 1.5. With help, though, he was able to demonstrate ability with the score 2.0 content and score 3.0 content. Therefore, his score is 1.0.

5. *Mr. Kitchens has created a role-play activity to assess his social studies students' knowledge about American presidents. He has provided directions for the role play, giving students three presidents from which to choose. After choosing one president, the students must create a scene that delivers personal facts about the president and the time in which he was in office (score 2.0 content). Students must also depict the president making one of his most influential choices (score 3.0 content). Finally, the scene must depict the president considering making a choice different from the one he made (score 4.0 content). Sally delivers the relevant information about the president she chose but depicts his character making a choice only the current president has encountered—not a choice her selected president had to make. She does not depict any other choices that the selected president could have made.*

Sally did not attempt the score 4.0 content and did not demonstrate mastery of the score 3.0 content at all. Since she did deliver correct facts about her chosen president, her score is 2.0.

Answers to Exercise 3.3

Review Questions

1. *What are some of the flaws of the 100-point scale?*

   One major flaw of the 100-point scale is the subjectivity in assigning points. Some teachers give more weight to items representing the simpler content, while others give more weight to items that address the more complex content (content not directly addressed in class). As a result, each teacher may grade the same assessment differently. In effect, this is like changing the length of an inch from one measurement to the next. A second flaw of the 100-point scale is that there are no criteria for answers that are partially correct. One teacher might give almost full credit for a partially correct answer, while another might give almost none.

2. *Describe the basic process for writing a scale.*

   Writing a scale begins with identifying a specific target learning goal. A target learning goal is the level of knowledge or skill the entire class will ideally achieve. To complete the scale, a goal defining more complex content and a goal defining simpler content than the target goal are written. The target learning goal represents score 3.0 content. The more complex content represents score 4.0 content, and the simpler content represents score 2.0. Scale scores 1.0 and 0.0 do not represent new content.

3. *Why is it important for students to rewrite scales in their own words?*

   One of the major advantages of defining clear learning goals and scales is that students will have a firm grasp of what they are expected to know or be able to do. It is much more likely that students have really considered and come to understand the goals when teachers give the class the opportunity to rewrite the scale(s) in their own words. Additionally, if students have access to scales written in language familiar to them, they can more easily propose student-generated assessments when they feel confident they can move up to a higher level of the scale.

4. *Describe how teachers can make use of preexisting assessments.*

   Using preexisting assessments is simply a matter of equating the items on the assessment to the scale scores. The simpler items would be equated to score 2.0, and the items that address the target learning goal would be equated to score 3.0 items. Items equivalent to score 4.0 may or may not appear on the assessment, and if they do not, teachers should modify the assessment to suit their purposes.

Answers to Exercise 4.1

Designing Selected-Response Assessment Tasks

1. One possible multiple-choice item might be the following:

   To which one of the following kingdoms do humans belong?

   A. Animalia

   B. Plantae

   C. Protista

   D. Fungi

   E. Monera

2. One possible matching item might be the following:

   Match the numbered event on the left with the date on which it occurred listed on the right.

1. D day _____	A. April 12, 1945
2. Hitler committed suicide _____	B. August 9, 1945
3. Bombing of Hiroshima _____	C. April 30, 1945
4. Bombing of Nagasaki _____	D. June 6, 1944
5. Truman becomes president of the U.S. _____	E. August 6, 1945
	F. October 8, 1946

3. One possible alternative-choice item might be the following:

   Which of the following is the correct formula for a quadratic equation?

   A. $ax^2 + bx + c = 0$

   B. $y = mx + b$

4. One possible true/false item might be the following:

   Mark the following statement with a *T* for true or an *F* for false.

   _____ Improvisation is an effective technique for improving stage presence.

5. One possible multiple-response item might be the following:

   Place a check in front of all fouls in the game of basketball.

   _____ Personal fouls

   _____ Technical fouls

_____ Offsides

_____ Intercepting

_____ Dunking

_____ Charging

6. One possible fill-in-the-blank item might be the following:

The human body needs _____ to fuel short, powerful bursts of movement, and the body uses _____, _____, and _____ to create that fuel.

Answers to Exercise 4.2

Designing Extended Constructed-Response Tasks and Demonstration Tasks

1. *Mathematics learning goal: Students will be able to make conversions between standard and nonstandard measurement systems.*

   A demonstration task seems the most straightforward way of assessing this learning goal. For example, a teacher might place three or four objects around the room and ask the students to measure each object in standard units. He or she would then ask them to sit down and independently convert the standard units to nonstandard units, showing their work. An essay option might be to provide students with a word problem. The problem gives measurements in standard units, and the answer asks for a final measurement in nonstandard units. The students must perform the necessary conversions, explaining their work.

2. *Science learning goal: Students will be able to discuss the water cycle and each of its stages.*

   This goal could be assessed with either a demonstration task or an essay task. If a teacher chose to use demonstration, he or she might ask students to create a physical model of the water cycle and explain its component parts. He or she might also ask students to show a portion of the water cycle through a demonstration of something like boiling water. The student would explain what is happening in the demonstration and what will happen next. An essay task might require the students to draw a graphic representation of the water cycle and explain in writing each stage and how the stages work together. The teacher could also ask students to write about real-life examples that illustrate each stage of the water cycle.

3. *Social studies learning goal: Students will be able to describe the events in a key battle from the Civil War and explain why either the Union or the Confederacy was the victor.*

   An essay task or a demonstration task would be appropriate for this learning goal. A demonstration might include asking students to create a physical model of a battle scene, use plastic game pieces to demonstrate the events of the battle, and explain how and why it was won by the Union or the Confederacy. An essay task might require students to write about two or three significant events in the battle in chronological order and then use those descriptions to explain the victory.

Answers to Exercise 4.3

Review Questions

1. *How are selected-response items and short constructed-response items typically used to design a paper/pencil test that addresses score 2.0, 3.0, and 4.0 content?*

   Because selected-response items require students only to recognize correct information that is presented to them, those items typically address score 2.0 content. Short constructed-response items can be used to ask students to demonstrate comprehension (typically score 3.0 content) or some form of analysis (typically score 4.0 content). When designing a paper/pencil test, the teacher would typically include one section with a few selected-response questions addressing score 2.0 content, another section with short constructed-response items addressing score 3.0 content, and a third section with short constructed-response items addressing score 4.0 content.

2. *Explain what you would do if a student demonstrated an aberrant pattern of responses in an assessment designed to address score 2.0, 3.0, and 4.0 content.*

   The first thing a teacher would do upon seeing an aberrant pattern of responses in an assessment would be to investigate whether or not an item or items were flawed. If flaws did exist, he or she could drop the item or items from the assessment. If the item or items were not flawed but were more difficult than initially thought, the teacher might reclassify the item or items as a higher or lower score value.

   The second thing a teacher would do upon seeing an aberrant pattern would be to consider the possibility that a student put effort into answering some of the items and not others. He or she would have a one-on-one conversation with the student and ask him or her to reconcile the issues on the assessment.

   The third thing a teacher might consider is the possibility that his or her evaluation of the item or items is in some way flawed. Consequently, the teacher would reexamine his or her scoring of the item or items.

3. *Explain why a well-constructed scale is critical to scoring a demonstration and unobtrusive observations.*

   Quite simply, if a scale is not well constructed, a teacher will not know what behaviors to look for in a demonstration or unobtrusive assessment. In other words, if the behaviors that demonstrate proficiency are not specified in the scale, a teacher has little option but to make subjective judgments about what behaviors constitute which score values. Furthermore, if the scale is not well constructed, students will not fully understand the learning goal and will not know what is expected of them.

Answers to Exercise 5.1

Record Keeping in the Four Approaches

1. *While using approach 1, a particular student exhibits the following pattern of formative scores for a particular learning goal: 2.0, 2.5, 3.0, 3.5, and 2.5. Describe how you would determine the student's summative score. Make sure to explain your reasoning.*

   Because this pattern of scores does not show a smooth upward trend, a teacher might reasonably sit down with the student and ask him or her about the variations and which score value he or she feels is appropriate. To provide evidence for the suggested summative score, the student might be asked to engage in a probing discussion and/or propose a student-generated assessment.

2. *Explain why the 100-point scale can be used with approach 3 but not with approach 1 or 2.*

   In approach 3, assessments focus on one level of content only—score 2.0, 3.0, or 4.0 content. Thus, the problem of different weights being applied to items that address different levels of content is alleviated, at least in part. As long as the teacher designs an assessment with a defined cut point or cut score that represents mastery of the content, the 100-point scale can be applied. If students' scores are higher than the cut point, the teacher can infer that the students have mastered the level of content (score 2.0, 3.0, or 4.0 content) for which the test was designed.

   In approaches 1 and 2, assessments will typically address all levels of the scale. As illustrated in the section in chapter 3 titled "The 100-Point Scale," when an assessment includes items at different levels of complexity regarding the scale content, the 100-point scale cannot appropriately reflect those differences.

3. *Explain why it is not a good idea to automatically use the last score in a set of formative scores as the summative score, even if the final score comes from a final examination.*

   Using the last score in a set of formative scores as the summative score ignores the inaccuracy inherent in any single assessment. Even if the final score comes from a final examination, error will still be present. The best way to eliminate or diminish error is to gather as much data from as many assessments as necessary to make a reasoned judgment about a student's true score.

4. *Explain why it is inappropriate to enter a score of 0 if a student misses an assessment or does not complete an assignment.*

   A student can be assigned a score of 0 only if he or she demonstrates no knowledge of a goal even with help from the teacher. In this case, a 0 would represent the student's true status. Missing or incomplete assignments are not evidence of knowledge or skill (or lack thereof), and so should not be treated as such.

Answers to Exercise 5.2
Review Questions

1. *What are the defining characteristics of approach 1?*

   There are two major defining characteristics of approach 1: the use of assessments with all score values on the scale from the very beginning of a unit, and the calculating of a summative score at the end of a grading period.

   The clear advantage to this approach is twofold: students know right away what they are expected to be able to know or do, and it is easy to track, and therefore celebrate, knowledge gain. The primary disadvantage to this approach is that it is nontraditional, and it may take some time for students and parents to become acclimated.

2. *What are the defining characteristics of approach 2?*

   There are two major defining characteristics of approach 2: a current summative score is kept at all times for every student, and though instruction begins with an assessment containing all score values of the scale, it is highly individualized after that point.

   The advantage of this approach is seated in its individualization. Students move at their own paces and can take control of their progress by using student-generated assessments. The major disadvantage to this approach is that because of the focus on individual students, it is labor-intensive.

3. *What are the defining characteristics of approach 3?*

   Approach 3 focuses on the class as a unit. Instead of addressing all score values for the scale on every assessment, this approach assesses each level of the scale separately. That is, students learn the score 2.0 content and are assessed on that first, and when the teacher is reasonably sure the class is ready to move on, score 3.0 content is addressed and assessed, and so on.

   The advantage to this approach lies in its similarity to traditional approaches. Students and parents will be familiar and comfortable with an approach that produces high scores on tests from the beginning. Additionally, the 100-point scale can be used here. The major disadvantage to this approach is that it does not address the individual needs of students very well.

4. *What are the defining characteristics of approach 4?*

   Approach 4 is defined by students' ability to increase their scores on any learning goal throughout the entire year. In this approach, students can track their formative scores on each assessment as well as track their summative scores across all learning goals.

   The advantage of this approach is that it greatly empowers students. The disadvantage is that it is nontraditional by nature and is quite labor-intensive.

5. Answers to question 5 will vary.

Answers to Exercise 6.1
Converting Scores

1. *Explain why it is legitimate to compute an average across summative scores for different learning goals but it is not legitimate to compute an average across formative scores within a given learning goal.*

It is not appropriate to compute an average across formative scores within a learning goal because the average does not take into account the fact that a student's scores will increase as he or she learns more about the goal. Averaging the scores within a learning goal would punish the student for low scores in the beginning of a grading period and would not be representative of his or her level of knowledge or skill at the end of the grading period. However, calculating an average for summative scores across learning goals is permissible because each learning goal has a unique focus. An average is a viable indicator of a student's overall "tendency" (central tendency) across a series of independent learning goals.

2A. *Using the conversion scale in table 6.1 (page 106), compute the letter grade for the student.*

Average score: 2.57

Grade: B-

2B. *Using the conversion scale in table 6.2 (page 109), translate the student's scores into one of the following categories: advanced, proficient, basic, or below basic.*

An average score of 2.57 translates into the proficient category.

2C. *Using the conversion scale in table 6.3 (page 110), translate the student's scores into an average percentage score.*

The average of 80% (2.5), 80% (2.5), 90% (3.0), 90% (3.0), 80% (2.5), 70% (2.0), and 80% (2.5) is 81.4%.

3. *For the seven summative scores used in question 2, assume that during the grading period, the teacher has addressed only score 2.0 content for goals 6 and 7 and just started score 3.0 content for goals 4 and 5. Devise a conjunctive approach that would take this into consideration, and compute a letter grade using the following matrix:*

	Minimum Score for A	Minimum Score for B	Minimum Score for C	Minimum Score for D	Score for F
Goal 1	3.0	2.5	2.0	1.0	0.5 or below
Goal 2	3.0	2.5	2.0	1.0	0.5 or below
Goal 3	3.0	2.5	2.0	1.0	0.5 or below
Goal 4	2.5	2.0	1.5	0.5	0.0
Goal 5	2.5	2.0	1.5	0.5	0.0
Goal 6	2.0	1.5	1.5	0.5	0.0
Goal 7	2.0	1.5	1.0	0.5	0.0

In this scenario, the teacher addressed score 2.0 content only for goals 6 and 7 during the grading period. Additionally, during the grading period, the teacher just began instruction in the score 3.0 content for goals 4 and 5. Therefore, it makes sense that the cut point or cut scores for a grade of an A would begin at 2.0 for goals 6 and 7 and at 2.5 for goals 4 and 5. This is reflected in the first column of the preceding matrix. The cut score for grades of B, C, D, and F is adjusted proportionally. The sample student received scores of 2.5, 2.5, 3.0, 3.0, 2.5, 2.0, and 2.5. For his or her first score of 2.5, the student does not meet the cut score for an A but does meet the cut score for a B; for the second score, he or she, again, meets the cut score for a B but not for an A. Comparing the student's obtained scores with the cut scores in the matrix, the student would receive a grade of B.

A major disadvantage of the conjunctive approach is that a single low score can dramatically change a student's grade. To illustrate, assume that the student's score on learning goal 1 was 2.0 instead of 2.5. As shown in the matrix, this low score would have dropped the student to a grade of C.

Formative Assessment and Standards-Based Grading • © 2010 Marzano Research Laboratory • marzanoresearch.com
Visit **marzanoresearch.com/classroomstrategiesthatwork** to download this page.

Answers to Exercise 6.2
Standards-Referenced Reporting

1. *Show how the student received an average score of 2.70 for working in groups.*

   The average of 2.70 for working in groups comes from averaging the following scores:

   Language arts score for working in groups: 3.0

   Mathematics score for working in groups: 2.0

   Science score for working in groups: 1.0

   Social studies score for working in groups: 4.0

   Art score for working in groups: 3.5

2. *Show how the student received an average score of 3.10 for social studies.*

   The score of 3.10 for social studies came from averaging the academic measurement topics for that subject area as follows:

   The influence of culture: 3.5

   Current events: 3.0

   Personal responsibility: 4.0

   Government representation: 3.5

   Human and civil rights: 1.5

3. *Identify the topic or topics for which the student exhibited the most gain over the grading period.*

   The student exhibited the most gain for the life skill of work completion in social studies. He or she went from a score of 1.0 to 3.5—a gain of 2.5 scale points. The student exhibited a gain of 2.0 scale points in the following areas:

   Analysis and evaluation of oral media in language arts

   Work completion in language arts

   Estimation in mathematics

   Multiplication/division in mathematics

   Behavior in mathematics

   Human identity in science

   Personal responsibility in social studies

   Government representation in social studies

Formative Assessment and Standards-Based Grading • © 2010 Marzano Research Laboratory • marzanoresearch.com
Visit **marzanoresearch.com/classroomstrategiesthatwork** to download this page.

Working in groups in social studies

Work completion in art

Working in groups in art

4. *Identify the topic or topics for which the student showed the least gain over the grading period.*

The language arts topic of literary analysis, the mathematics topic of ratio/proportion/percent, and the science topic of matter and energy all showed no gain.

Answers to Exercise 6.3

Standards-Based Reporting

1. *In table 6.6 (page 119), explain what "3 of 36" for level 4 in language arts means.*

   The notation "3 of 36" means that the student has reached proficiency (score 3.0 or higher) in three of the thirty-six learning goals for language arts.

2. *In table 6.6, explain why art and technology have fewer levels than the other subject areas.*

   Table 6.6 depicts a standards-based system that uses levels instead of grades. Because content is not split up into age-based grades, the nature of the content divides the levels. Some subject areas will have more levels than others.

3. *Explain why an overall grade cannot be assigned in a standards-based approach.*

   A standards-based approach either uses performance levels instead of grade levels or treats grade levels as performance levels. As such, students do not move up until they have demonstrated mastery on all of the learning goals at a specific level. The reporting practices in a standards-based system are different. Instead of overall letter grades that represent the average performance in the content addressed at a given grade level, teachers and students keep track of how many learning goals students have demonstrated mastery of in a particular subject area at a particular level. Given that students might be working at one level in mathematics, another level in science, and still another in language arts, there is no useful way to report grades for subject areas. The more relevant information is how many learning goals have been mastered for a specific subject at a specific level.

4. *Explain how the "grade-level" standards-based approach differs from the standards-based approach that does not use grade levels.*

   In grades K–8, the grade-level standards-based approach looks nearly identical to the pure performance-level standards-based approach. Students move from one level (grade level or pure performance level) only when they have demonstrated mastery for all of the learning goals in their current level. At the high school level, however, a grade-level standards-based approach uses specific courses instead of levels. For the grade-level approach, students must demonstrate mastery of the learning goals in the courses with simpler or more basic content before they move on to courses with more complex or difficult content. For example, in mathematics, Algebra I addresses simpler content than Algebra II, and so on. Once a student has demonstrated mastery (score 3.0 content) for all of the learning goals within a course, he or she receives credit for that course and moves on to another course.

APPENDIX B

WHAT IS AN EFFECT SIZE?

Reports on educational research use terms such as *meta-analysis* and *effect size* (ES). While these terms are without doubt useful to researchers, they can be confusing and even frustrating for the practitioner. So what does meta-analysis mean exactly? What is an ES? A meta-analysis is a summary, or synthesis, of relevant research findings. It looks at all of the individual studies done on a particular topic and summarizes them. This is helpful to educators in that a meta-analysis provides more and stronger support than does a single analysis (meta-analysis is literally an analysis of analyses).

An average ES tells us about the results across all of the individual studies examined. For example, let us say the purpose of the meta-analysis is to examine multiple studies regarding the effect of formative assessment on student achievement (that is, the effect of X on Y). An average ES reports the results of all of the included studies to tell us whether or not formative assessment improves student achievement and, if so, by how much.

Exactly how does a meta-analysis work, and how is an ES calculated? Empirical research is highly detailed and often uses idiomatic language; however, in the following steps, we have made efforts to demystify the processes of meta-analysis and ES calculation.

1. *Researchers survey the wide field of educational studies available with an eye for what is relevant to their meta-analysis.* They create keyword lists to help determine the breadth and depth of the search. Published articles, unpublished articles, dissertations, book chapters, and online and other electronic databases are considered for inclusion. Quite simply, they construct a database of all relevant studies.

2. *After an initial examination of the relevant studies, researchers have an idea of the rigor of each study. They craft their own inclusion criteria by asking which studies are good enough to include and which studies should be excluded.* They also pay close attention to the similarities and differences between the studies. Strong results will be based on studies with common purposes and variables. In other words, researchers want to include the

studies that are most analogous. For example, if one study defines student achievement in terms of standardized test scores, and another defines student achievement in terms of students' self-reported learning, researchers would probably not include both studies in the same meta-analysis.

3. *Once researchers have identified the studies they will use for a meta-analysis, they examine the results of each study.* Specifically, they look at the ESs of each study in order to mathematically calculate an average ES for the overall meta-analysis. The process behind calculating the ES is quite detailed, but basically it is computed by determining the difference between the mean of the experimental group (the group that has had the benefit of a particular educational practice), and the mean of the control group (the group that has not had the benefit of a particular educational practice), and then dividing the difference by the standard deviation. In simple terms, a standard deviation is the average distance each score is from the mean. For example, if the mean of a group of scores is 60, and the standard deviation is 5, then the average distance each score is from 60 is 5.

To illustrate how an ES is computed, let us assume that one class of science students is the experimental group; their class received formative assessments and took a test on the science content addressed during a specific unit. Another class served as the control group; those students did not receive formative assessments for that unit and took the same test. The experimental group had a mean (average) score of 85 on the test, and the control group had a mean score of 75. The standard deviation for the test given to both groups was 20. The ES for this study would be 0.50 [(85 − 75)/20]. This means that the average score in the experimental group is 0.50 of a standard deviation larger than the mean score of the control group.

An advantage of the ES is that it can be readily and accurately interpreted in terms of average percentile gain. A percentile gain effectively translates an ES into a language we can understand. Just how this is done requires a somewhat detailed explanation. Briefly though, an ES is equivalent to a point on the normal distribution, and once you have a point on the normal distribution, you can determine the expected percentile gain (or loss) for someone at the 50th percentile. Table A.1 lists expected percentile gains for various ESs. If the ES for formative assessment is 0.50, for example, a teacher could predict that students in the classroom will improve by 19 percentile points. That is, students scoring at the 50th percentile on achievement tests would be predicted to score at the 69th percentile after formative assessment had been introduced. In general, the higher the ES, the better.

When an average effect size for an educational practice is calculated using a number of studies in a meta-analysis, practitioners can be even more sure that the average ES and its associated percentile gain are accurate. Although terms such as *meta-analysis, average effect size,* and *percentile gain* may look daunting at first, they are ultimately employed to gather the widest array of the strongest research and translate the findings into meaningful language for the classroom teacher or school administrator.

Table A.1 Conversion of Effect Size to Percentile Gain

Effect Size	Percentile Gain	Effect Size	Percentile Gain	Effect Size	Percentile Gain	Effect Size	Percentile Gain
				0.5	19		
0.01	0	0.26	10	0.51	19	0.76	28
0.02	1	0.27	11	0.52	20	0.77	28
0.03	1	0.28	11	0.53	20	0.78	28
0.04	2	0.29	11	0.54	21	0.79	29
0.05	2	0.3	12	0.55	21	0.8	29
0.06	2	0.31	12	0.56	21	0.81	29
0.07	3	0.32	13	0.57	22	0.82	29
0.08	3	0.33	13	0.58	22	0.83	30
0.09	4	0.34	13	0.59	22	0.84	30
0.1	4	0.35	14	0.6	23	0.85	30
0.11	4	0.36	14	0.61	23	0.86	31
0.12	5	0.37	14	0.62	23	0.87	31
0.13	5	0.38	15	0.63	24	0.88	31
0.14	6	0.39	15	0.64	24	0.89	31
0.15	6	0.4	16	0.65	24	0.9	32
0.16	6	0.41	16	0.66	25	0.91	32
0.17	7	0.42	16	0.67	25	0.92	32
0.18	7	0.43	17	0.68	25	0.93	32
0.19	8	0.44	17	0.69	25	0.94	33
0.2	8	0.45	17	0.7	26	0.95	33
0.21	8	0.46	18	0.71	26	0.96	33
0.22	9	0.47	18	0.72	26	0.97	33
0.23	9	0.48	18	0.73	27	0.98	34
0.24	9	0.49	19	0.74	27	0.99	34
0.25	10			0.75	27		

Continued on next page →

Effect Size	Percentile Gain	Effect Size	Percentile Gain	Effect Size	Percentile Gain	Effect Size	Percentile Gain
1	34			1.5	43		
1.01	34	1.26	40	1.51	43	1.76	46
1.02	35	1.27	40	1.52	44	1.77	46
1.03	35	1.28	40	1.53	44	1.78	46
1.04	35	1.29	40	1.54	44	1.79	46
1.05	35	1.3	40	1.55	44	1.8	46
1.06	36	1.31	40	1.56	44	1.81	46
1.07	36	1.32	41	1.57	44	1.82	47
1.08	36	1.33	41	1.58	44	1.83	47
1.09	36	1.34	41	1.59	44	1.84	47
1.1	36	1.35	41	1.6	45	1.85	47
1.11	37	1.36	41	1.61	45	1.86	47
1.12	37	1.37	41	1.62	45	1.87	47
1.13	37	1.38	42	1.63	45	1.88	47
1.14	37	1.39	42	1.64	45	1.89	47
1.15	37	1.4	42	1.65	45	1.90	47
1.16	38	1.41	42	1.66	45	1.91	47
1.17	38	1.42	42	1.67	45	1.92	47
1.18	38	1.43	42	1.68	45	1.93	47
1.19	38	1.44	43	1.69	45	1.94	47
1.2	38	1.45	43	1.7	46	1.95	47
1.21	39	1.46	43	1.71	46	1.96	48
1.22	39	1.47	43	1.72	46	1.97	48
1.23	39	1.48	43	1.73	46	1.98	48
1.24	39	1.49	43	1.74	46	1.99	48
1.25	39			1.75	46		

Note: Effect sizes over 2.00 correspond to percentile gains of 49%.

REFERENCES

Azevedo, R., & Bernard, R. (1995). Assessing the effects of feedback in computer-assisted learning. *British Journal of Educational Technology, 26*(1), 57–58.

Baker, E. L., Aschbacher, P. R., Niemi, D., & Sato, E. (1992). *CRESST performance assessment models: Assessing content area explanations.* Los Angeles: University of California, National Center for Research on Evaluation, Standards, and Student Testing.

Baldwin, J. (1884). *Art of school management.* New York: D. Appleton.

Bangert-Drowns, R. L., Kulik, C. C., Kulik, J. A., & Morgan, M. (1991). The instructional effects of feedback in test-like events. *Review of Educational Research, 61,* 213–238.

Bangert-Drowns, R. L., Kulik, J. A., & Kulik, C. C. (1991). Effects of frequent classroom testing. *Journal of Educational Research, 85*(2), 89–99.

Black, P., & Wiliam, D. (1998a). Assessment and classroom learning. *Assessment in Education, 5*(1), 7–75.

Black, P., & Wiliam, D. (1998b). Inside the black box: Raising standards through classroom assessment. *Phi Delta Kappan, 80*(2). Accessed at www.pdkintl.org/kappan/kbla9810.htm on May 5, 2009.

Bloom, B. S. (1976). *Human characteristics and school learning.* New York: McGraw-Hill.

Bloom, B. S., Madaus, G. F., & Hastings, J. T. (1981). *Evaluation to improve learning.* New York: McGraw-Hill.

Boscardin, C. K., Jones, B., Nishimura, C., Madsen, S., & Park, J.-E. (2008). *Assessment of content understanding through science explanation tasks* (CRESST Report 745). Los Angeles: University of California Graduate School of Education and Information Studies, National Center for Research on Evaluation, Standards, and Student Testing (CRESST).

Brookhart, S. (2004). *Grading.* Upper Saddle River, NJ: Pearson Education.

Brookhart, S., & Nitko, A. (2007). *Assessment and grading in classrooms.* Upper Saddle River, NJ: Pearson Education.

Burns, M. K. (2004). Empirical analysis of drill ratio research: Refining the instructional level for drill tasks. *Remedial and Special Education, 25*(3), 167–173.

Burns, M. K., & Symington, T. (2002). A meta-analysis of preferential intervention teams: Student and systemic outcomes. *Journal of School Psychology, 40*, 437–447.

Chidester, T. R., & Grigsby, W. C. (1984). A meta-analysis of the goal setting–performance literature. *Academy of Management Proceedings, 35*, 202–206.

Cizek, G. (2007). Formative classroom and large-scale assessment: Implications for future research and development. In J. H. McMillan (Ed.), *Formative classroom assessment* (pp. 99–115). New York: Teachers College Press.

Cross, L., & Frary, R. (1999). Hodgepodge grading: Endorsed by students and teachers alike. *Applied Measurement in Education, 12,* 53–72.

DeLorenzo, R. A., Battino, W. J., Schreiber, R. M., & Gaddy-Carrio, B. (2009). *Delivering on the promise: The education revolution.* Bloomington, IN: Solution Tree Press.

Durm, M. W. (1993, Spring). An A is not an A is not an A: A history of grading. *The Educational Forum, 57,* 294–297.

Fraser, B. J., Walberg, H. J., Welch, W. W., & Hattie, J. A. (1987). Synthesis of educational productivity research [Special issue]. *International Journal of Educational Research, 11*(2), 145–252.

Fuchs, L. S., & Fuchs, D. (1986). Effects of systematic formative evaluation: A meta-analysis. *Exceptional Children, 53*(3), 199–208.

Gocmen, G. (2003). Effectiveness of frequent testing over academic achievement: A meta-analysis study. *Dissertation Abstracts International, 64*(7), 2402A. (UMI No. 3099579)

Gollwitzer, P. M., & Sheeran, P. (2006). Implementation intentions and goal achievement: A meta-analysis of effects and processes. *Advances in Experimental Social Psychology, 38,* 69–119.

Graham, S., & Perin, D. (2007). A meta-analysis of writing instruction for adolescent students. *Journal of Educational Psychology, 99,* 445–476.

Guskey, T. (2009). *Practical solutions for serious problems in standards-based grading.* Thousand Oaks, CA: Corwin Press.

Guskey, T., & Bailey, J. (2001). *Developing grading and reporting systems for student learning.* Thousand Oaks, CA: Corwin Press.

Haas, M. (2005). Teaching methods for secondary algebra: A meta-analysis of findings. *NASSP Bulletin, 89*(642), 24–46.

Haller, E. P., Child, D. A., & Walberg, H. J. (1988). Can comprehension be taught? A quantitative synthesis of "metacognitive studies." *Educational Researcher, 17*(9), 5–8.

Haponstall, K. (2009). *An analysis of the correlation between standards-based, non-standards-based grading systems and achievement as measured by the Colorado student assessment program (CSAP).* Unpublished doctoral dissertation, Capella University, Minneapolis, MN.

Hattie, J. (1999, August). *Influences on student learning* (Inaugural professorial address, University of Auckland, New Zealand). Accessed at www.teacherstoolbox.CO.UK/downloads/managers/Influencesonstudent.pdf on August 12, 2009.

Hattie, J. (2003). *Formative and summative interpretations of assessment information.* Accessed at www.education.auckland.ac.nz/uoa/fms/default/education/staff/Prof.%20John%20Hattie/ Documents/John%20Hattie%20Papers/assessment/Formative%20and%20Summative%20 Assessment%20(2003).pdf on April 13, 2009.

Hattie, J. (2009). *Visible learning: A synthesis of over 800 meta-analyses relating to achievement.* New York: Routledge.

Hattie, J., & Timperley, H. (2007). The power of feedback. *Review of Educational Research, 77,* 81–112.

Hausknecht, J. P., Halpert, J. A., DiPaolo, N. T., & Gerrard, M. O. M. (2007). Retesting in selection: A meta-analysis of coaching and practice effects for tests of cognitive ability. *Journal of Applied Psychology, 92,* 373–385.

Heritage, M. (2008). *Learning progressions: Supporting instruction and formative assessment.* Washington, DC: Council of Chief State School Officers.

Heritage, M., Kim, J., Vendlinski, T. P., & Herman, J. L. (2008). *From evidence to action: A seamless process in formative assessment?* (CRESST Report 741). Los Angeles: University of California Graduate School of Education and Information Studies, National Center for Research on Evaluation, Standards, and Student Testing (CRESST).

Herman, J. L., & Choi, K. (2008, August). *Formative assessment and the improvement of middle school science learning: The role of teacher advocacy* (CRESST Report 740). Los Angeles: University of California Graduate School of Education and Information Studies, National Center for Research on Evaluation, Standards, and Student Testing (CRESST).

Kim, S.-E. (2005). *Effects of implementing performance assessments on student learning: Meta-analysis using HLM.* Unpublished doctoral dissertation, Pennsylvania State University.

Kluger, A. N., & DeNisi, A. (1996). The effects of feedback interventions on performance: A historical review, a meta-analysis, and a preliminary feedback intervention theory. *Psychological Bulletin, 119*(2), 254–284.

Kulik, J., Kulik, C., & Bangert-Drowns, R. L. (1984, April). *Effects of computer-based education on elementary school pupils.* Paper presented at the annual meeting of the American Educational Research Association, New Orleans, LA.

Kumar, D. D. (1991). A meta-analysis of the relationship between science instruction and student engagement. *Education Review, 43*(1), 49–66.

Lang, D. (2007). Class rank, GPA, and valedictorians: How high schools rank students. *American Secondary Education, 35*(2), 36–48.

Lee, J. (2006, April). *Is test-driven external accountability effective? A meta-analysis of the evidence from cross-state causal-comparative and correlational studies.* Paper presented at the annual meeting of the American Educational Research Association, San Francisco, CA.

Lipsey, M. W., & Wilson, D. B. (1993). The efficacy of psychological, educational, and behavioral treatment. *American Psychologist, 48,* 1181–1209.

Locke, E. A., & Latham, G. P. (1990). *A theory of goal setting and task performance.* Englewood Cliffs, NJ: Prentice Hall.

Locke, E. A., & Latham, G. P. (2002). Building a practically useful theory of goal setting and task motivation. *American Psychologist, 57,* 705–717.

Lou, Y., Abrami, P. C., Spence, J. C., Paulsen, C., Chambers, B., & d'Apollonio, S. (1996). Within-class grouping: A meta-analysis. *Review of Educational Research, 66,* 423–458.

Lysakowski, R. S., & Walberg, H. J. (1981). Classroom reinforcement in relation to learning: A quantitative analysis. *Journal of Educational Research, 75,* 69–77.

Lysakowski, R. S., & Walberg, H. J. (1982). Instructional effects of cues, participation, and corrective feedback: A quantitative synthesis. *American Educational Research Journal, 19,* 559–578.

Marzano Research Laboratory. (2009). *Tracking student progress and scoring scales.* Accessed at http://files .solution-tree.com/MRL/documents/stid20_summaryreport.pdf on September 21, 2009.

Marzano, R. J. (2002). A comparison of selected methods of scoring classroom assessments. *Applied Measurement in Education, 15,* 249–268.

Marzano, R. J. (2006). *Classroom assessment and grading that work.* Alexandria, VA: Association for Supervision and Curriculum and Development.

Marzano, R. J. (2007). *The art and science of teaching: A comprehensive framework for effective instruction.* Alexandria, VA: Association for Supervision and Curriculum and Development.

Marzano, R. J. (2009). *Designing and teaching learning goals and objectives: Classroom strategies that work.* Bloomington, IN: Marzano Research Laboratory.

Marzano, R. J., & Haystead, M. W. (2008). *Making standards useful in the classroom.* Alexandria, VA: Association for Supervision and Curriculum and Development.

Marzano, R. J., Pickering, D., & Pollock, J. (2001). *Classroom instruction that works.* Alexandria, VA: Association for Supervision and Curriculum and Development.

Marzano, R. J., & Waters, T. (2009). *District leadership that works: Striking the right balance.* Bloomington, IN: Solution Tree Press and Mid-continent Research for Education and Learning.

McMillan, J. H. (Ed.). (2007). *Formative classroom assessment: Theory into practice.* New York: Teachers College, Columbia University.

Menges, R. J., & Brinko, K. T. (1986, April). *Effects of student evaluation feedback: A meta-analysis of higher education research.* Paper presented at the annual meeting of the American Educational Research Association, San Francisco, CA.

Mento, A. J., Steel, R. P., & Karren, R. J. (1987). A meta-analytic study of the effects of goal setting on task performance: 1966–1984. *Organizational Behavior and Human Decision Processes, 39*(1), 52–83.

Moin, A. K. (1986). *Relative effectiveness of various techniques of calculus instruction: A meta-analysis.* Unpublished doctoral dissertation, University of Syracuse, Syracuse, New York.

National Education Goals Panel. (1993, November). *Promises to keep: Creating high standards for American students.* A report on the review of education standards from the Goal 3 and 4 Technical Planning Group to the National Education Goals Panel. Washington DC: Author.

Neubert, M. J. (1998). The value of feedback and goal setting over goal setting alone and potential moderators of this effect: A meta-analysis. *Human Performance, 11*(4), 321–335.

O'Connor, K. (2002). *How to grade for learning.* Arlington Heights, IL: SkyLight Professional Development.

Pellegrino, J. W., Chudowsky, N., & Glaser, W. (Eds.). (2001). *Knowing what students know: The science and design of educational assessment.* Washington, DC: National Academy Press.

Popham, W. J. (2003). *Test better, teach better: The instructional role of assessment.* Alexandria, VA: Association for Supervision and Curriculum Development.

Popham, W. J. (2006). Phony formative assessments: Buyer beware. *Educational Leadership, 64*(3), 86–87.

Popham, W. J. (2008). *Transformative assessment.* Alexandria, VA: Association for Supervision and Curriculum Development.

Reeves, D. B. (2004, December). The case against the zero. *Phi Delta Kappan, 86*(4), 324–325.

Scriven, M. (1967). The methodology of evaluation. In R. F. Stake (Ed.), *Curriculum evaluation: American Educational Research Association monograph series on evaluation,* No. 1 (pp. 39–83). Chicago: Rand McNally.

Shepard, L. (2006, June). *Integrating assessment with instruction: What will it take to make it work?* Panelist presentation delivered at the National Large-Scale Assessment Conference sponsored by the Council of Chief State School Officers, San Francisco, CA.

Shute, V. J. (2008). Focus on formative feedback. *Review of Educational Research, 78,* 153–189.

Stiggins, R., Arter, J., Chappuis, J., & Chappuis, S. (2006). *Classroom assessment for student learning: Doing it right—Using it well.* Princeton, NJ: Merrill Prentice Hall with Educational Testing Service.

Swanson, H. L., & Lussier, C. M. (2001). A selective synthesis of the experimental literature on dynamic assessment. *Review of Educational Research, 71,* 321–363.

Tenenbaum, G., & Goldring, E. (1989). A meta-analysis of the effect of enhanced instruction: Cues, participation, reinforcement, and feedback and correctives on motor skill learning. *Journal of Research and Development in Education, 22*(3), 53–64.

Travlos, A. K., & Pratt, J. (1995). Temporal locus of knowledge of results: A meta-analytic review. *Perceptual and Motor Skills, 80*(1), 3–14.

Tubbs, M. E. (1986). Goal setting: A meta-analytic examination of the empirical evidence. *Journal of Applied Psychology, 71,* 474–483.

Walberg, H. J. (1999). Productive teaching. In H. C. Waxman & H. J. Walberg (Eds.), *New directions for teaching practice research* (pp. 75–104). Berkley, CA: McCutchen.

Washington Office of Superintendent of Public Instruction. (2008, July). *Washington State K–12 Mathematics Learning Standards.* Accessed at www.k12.wa.us/CurriculumInstruct/Mathematics/pubdocs/K-12MathematicsStandards-July2008.pdf on September 3, 2009.

Welsh, M. E., & D'Agostino, J. V. (2009). Fostering consistency between standards-based grades and large-scale assessment results. In T. R. Guskey (Ed.), *Practical solutions for serious problems in standards-based grading* (pp. 75–104). Thousand Oaks, CA: Corwin Press.

Wiggins, G. (1993, November). Assessment: Authenticity, context, and validity. *Phi Delta Kappan, 75*(3), 200–214.

Wiggins, G. (1996). Honesty and fairness: Toward better grading and reporting. In T. R. Guskey (Ed.), *ASCD yearbook, 1996: Communicating student learning* (pp. 141–177). Alexandria, VA: Association for Supervision and Curriculum Development.

Wiliam, D., & Leahy, S. (2007). A theoretical foundation for formative assessment. In J. H. McMillan (Ed.), *Formative classroom assessment* (pp. 29–42). New York: Teachers College Press.

Wise, K. C., & Okey, J. R. (1983). A meta-analysis of the effects of various science teaching strategies on achievement. *Journal of Research in Science Teaching, 20*(5), 415–425.

Witt, P. L., Wheeless, L. R., & Allen, M. (2006). A relationship between teacher immediacy and student learning: A meta-analysis. In B. M. Gayle, R. W. Preiss, N. Burrell, & M. Allen (Eds.), *Classroom communication and instructional process: Advances through meta-analysis* (pp. 149–168). Mahwah, NJ: Lawrence Erlbaum.

Wood, R. E., Mento, A. J., & Locke, E. A. (1987). Task complexity as a moderator of goal effects: A meta-analysis. *Journal of Applied Psychology, 72,* 416–425.

Wright, P. M. (1990). Operationalization of goal difficulty as a moderator of the goal difficulty-performance relationship. *Journal of Applied Psychology, 72,* 227–234.

Yeany, R. H., & Miller, P. A. (1983). Effects of diagnostic/remedial instruction on science learning: A meta-analysis. *Journal of Research in Science Teaching, 20,* 19–26.

Yeh, S. S. (2008). The cost-effectiveness of comprehensive school reform and rapid assessment. *Education Policy Analysis Archives, 16*(13). Accessed at http://epas.asu.edu/epaa/v16n13/ on June 30, 2008.

INDEX